Politics,
Power,
Polls,
and
School
Elections

Michael Y. Nunnery
Professor of Educational Administration
University of Florida

Ralph B. Kimbrough
Chairman, Department of
Educational Administration
University of Florida

McCutchan Publishing Corporation
2526 Grove Street
Berkeley, California 94704

campaigns, with special reference to school elections, illustrated by a detailed review of the workings of an actual referendum.

The authors have used the local school district as the primary focus of political activity. The material is equally useful, however, in state referenda. Although the state is a more highly complex political system than the local school district, the concepts, approaches, and nuts-and-bolts political techniques discussed are applicable to both. And success in statewide elections depends upon viable organization at the local political level.

Politics, Power, Polls, and School Elections is a book created from the fusion of sophisticated research and empirical knowledge. It may be used in college and university training programs for school administrators. However, school superintendents, board members, central office personnel, and other school leaders will also find the book helpful.

Michael Y. Nunnery
Ralph B. Kimbrough

Gainesville, Florida

Contents

1

A Point of View

In this chapter a rational basis is developed for the knowledgeable involvement of school leaders in political activity. Stress is placed upon the meaning of politics, the continuous nature of political leadership, the changing concept of educational administration, and the importance of elections to educational opportunity.

Politics Defined

Unfortunately, the terms "politics" and "politician" have negative connotations to many educators. If a school official does not like a particular governmental decision, he may blame it on "politics." In the past, most self-respecting school administrators were horrified at the prospect of being labeled "politicians" by their colleagues. These attitudes, legacies from a variety of sources, became crystallized for a time in our professional lore. Yet the terms "politics" and "politician," according to the dictionary, refer to the art or science of governing. Since when has leadership in the art or science of governing become unprofessional?

Used appropriately, politics is the democratic process of making significant decisions in the school district, the state, and the nation. Each time educators or lay leaders take action to influence educational policy, or policies in other areas of society, they are involved in politics. Thus, educational leadership to upgrade educational standards is political. And if educators and citizens desire changes in school programs, they must be good politicians. Performing as a politician to develop quality schools is a perfectly legitimate, statesmanlike activity.

Distinguished educators have traditionally provided leadership in organized political activity. On close examination, we find that we have been more engaged in political activity than we usually realize. The well-organized school public relations program, the citizens' committees, cooperative school surveys, and other forms of citizen involvement are all political activities. If educators assess their activities realistically, they will find that political leadership equates with professional leadership in influencing public opinion.

This book is not written with the "Machiavellian" idea of outwitting or deceiving the citizen into accepting educators' values. *The educational statesman cannot separate his personal morality from the morality of political practice.* He does not engage in shady deals or political patronage. His political actions should exemplify the valued traditions of democracy, and he should provide effective, statesman-like leadership in the political system.

The patrons of the schools have a right to expect their educational leaders (both lay and professional) to use modern political techniques. That is, educators should be effective politicians. Otherwise, the views of those citizens favoring quality schools will not receive adequate consideration in the political processes of the school district, state, and nation.

Political Leadership, a Continuous Process

The exercise of political leadership is an ongoing process, not a role assumed only during elections. Successful use of the election process to produce quality schools depends on the continuous participation of school leaders in all significant aspects of the political system. For example, by the time propositions are submitted to the electorate they have already been shaped to the satisfaction of powerful persons and groups. We have all heard voters speak in frustrated terms of "voting for the lesser evil" among the candidates for office. Democracy has not progressed to the point where voters make direct decisions. They are usually forced to approve or disapprove decisions made by others, not all of whom are their elected representatives. A hidebound board of education may win all the elections it conducts yet have mediocre schools because it does not bring to a vote those propositions that would produce a breakthrough for quality schools. Schoolmen must not only win elections, but also influence the decisions of men in power to submit significant alternatives to referenda.

This kind of influence comes from active participation in the political system. School officials must build political influence for education. They must understand the political system and the exercise of political power in decisionmaking. They must earn respect in that system through their involvement and eventual leadership.

The Leadership Function

Educational administration is rapidly moving toward a new concept of the leadership function. Many educators no longer emphasize their executive function of carrying out policies given to them by a "nonpartisan" board of education. They see the need for their dynamic leadership of board members and the citizens of the community in building a quality education system. Furthermore, modern administrators are not preoccupied with keeping equilibrium in the educational and political systems. Realizing that progressive changes may produce stress and disequilibrium, they learn to survive with the stresses, the controversies, and the tumultuous conditions that accompany progress.

There is no "business as usual" when laymen and educators furnish leadership in the political arena. The world of politics is full of unexpected events and conditions. In its practical application, politics is an art. Therefore, it is essential for school officials to understand the political arena, and to learn how to be successful in influencing the system.

Internal conflicts between practicing school administrators and school board members have arisen concerning the political nature of schools. Traditionally, the process of educational administration was based on the idea, stemming from governmental reform, that the schools should be insulated from politics. The counter idea is that the people have the right — indeed the obligation — to exercise political pressure to influence the policies by which schools are operated. The latter view obviously subjects the schools to cross-pressures from the community, because the general public rarely achieves consensus on the purposes of schools. Clearly the schools cannot remain both insulated from the public and operated in accordance with the conflicting power interests of the citizens. A choice must be made.

The authors do not accept the insulated version of school administration. Practice of the concept results in a very conservative, sterile

educational system. Those who say that the schools are insulated from politics are using an obsolete slogan. The school system should be characterized by a high degree of openness. It should find ways for potent interaction and communication with its suprasystem, the community. One of the tragedies of schools in many districts is the breakdown of communication with the citizens served, including students. The school that attempts to build complete insulation from other sectors of the community either will not survive or will be unable to fulfill its purposes in a democratic society. Schools cannot afford to be free of politics. Neither should they be limited by ineffective political activity.

Winning School Elections

Education officials need to furnish leadership in school elections. They must organize politically to support school bond elections, school millage elections, consolidation proposals, and other referenda affecting educational policies in the district. They should also provide political direction in statewide referenda whenever the improvement of education in all school districts of the state depends on a favorable outcome.

An unsuccessful election reduces educational opportunities for students. Most educators are aware that failure of a bond election will downgrade education by forcing overcrowded conditions, double sessions, and other improvisations for lack of adequate resources. Poor morale among school personnel, parents, and students often follows defeated millage and capital construction elections, and several defeated school elections can impede the economic and social development of a city.

Each year an alarmingly high number of school bond elections are defeated in the United States. Of equal or possibly greater significance is the fact that leaders of many school districts are reluctant to call for bond elections or ask for higher millage levies lest they fail to be approved by the electorate. A respected superintendent of schools, confronted with the need for more funds in one of the largest school systems in the United States, noted that the sensible thing to do in his district would be to pass a bond issue and start construction of school facilities as recommended in a recently conducted survey. However, in his opinion the sensible course of action could not be followed. He felt that the schools of his district would

have to go on double sessions before the people would approve a bond issue.

Is it as impossible to influence the electorate as the superintendent implies? The authors do not believe that schools must become degraded before the public will accept responsibility for maintaining quality instruction. If educators provide effective political influence, most citizens will support quality schools. Such support will not arise in a spontaneous ground swell; educators will have to provide vigorous political leadership to earn it.

The quality of public education in the United States is related to the ability of school leaders to influence the political system within which the schools function. The authors believe that public opinion is the result rather than the basis of political activity, and schoolmen can influence public opinion through their own political activity.

Considerable evidence discloses that the educational policies of school districts are not dictated by socioeconomic conditions. An analysis of 122 school districts in four states indicated very little consistent relationship between socioeconomic factors (i.e., income, unemployment, density of population, age of population, and about 20 other measures) and school fiscal policies.[1] This study indicated that the kind of political system in which schools function may be a potent factor in limiting educational policies. The quality of education is related to the maturity of the political system served (i.e., the extent to which the system is open to the emergence of new leadership and ideas) and the ability of school officials to exercise leadership in influencing the system. Thus, effective political activity by schoolmen will improve school quality whatever the socioeconomic background of the school district may be.

Nonschool Elections

The destiny of schools is tied inextricably to the destiny of the larger society. School elections are not the only elections of concern to school leaders. The election process influences resolution of issues and establishment of policies in all areas of community living. Through it, persons are selected to set community policies; decisions are affirmed to build hospitals, float street bonds, provide for industrial expansion, extend municipal boundaries, establish planning, and undertake a host of other civic endeavors. Thus, the general election process influences the kind of community the schools serve, and the

general policies set for community living influence policies set for the schools.

Studies have shown a relationship between identifiable community behavior and educational development. For example, if the political system is conservative, we would not expect ready acceptance of liberal policies for the public schools. Again, the decision of a group of businessmen to build a multimillion-dollar factory in the school district cannot be treated with indifference by school leaders, because it inevitably places a greater burden on the schools to serve an expanded population.

Since the quality of education in the school system is related to the maturity of the larger political system served, educators experience great difficulty in operating healthy schools under a politically "sick" power structure. Consequently, educators' leadership in politics cannot be restricted to school elections. They need to be active leaders in the broad range of civic affairs in the school district.

How deeply should educators be involved in nonschool elections? Should they become involved in a decision concerning bonding authority to build a commercial airport? Should they leave to physicians the leadership for establishing a new health facility? Do they have a professional or only a personal interest in tax assessment policies and law enforcement practices? There are no definitive answers to these questions. They can only be answered within the complex context of each particular school district.

There do appear to be reasons for educators to exercise greater interest and participation in general civic affairs than traditional practice demanded. The fostering of excellence in education requires school leaders to give attention to general community conditions beyond the routine operation of schools. And school officials can build a broader base of influence for educational development by participative cooperation in the wide range of civic developments.

Footnotes

1. Roe L. Johns and Ralph B. Kimbrough, *The Relationship of Socioeconomic Factors, Educational Leadership Patterns and Elements of Community Power Structure to Local Fiscal Policy* (Washington: U.S. Department of Health, Education, and Welfare, Office of Education, Bureau of Research, Cooperative Research Project No. 2842, 1968).

2

Understanding the Political System

In organizing school elections, educational leaders must understand the political system (or power structure) of the school district. Leaders within this system have great influence on the opinions of many voters. If enough of these community leaders support the school proposal to be voted on, its chances of passage by the electorate are greatly enhanced. Conversely, their opposition can mean disaster for the proposal. Within the political system (or systems) encompassed by the school district, there are formal and informal groups through which an educator's influence on voter opinion is maximized. School election campaigns should be based on an accurate understanding of the political groupings. This chapter discusses what has been learned about the power structures of school districts and the steps a school leader may take to understand the power structure of his particular district.

The school system is administered within a complex power structure. The typical board of education does not exercise final authority over educational policies. In reality it exercises power only to the extent that it can legitimize its decisions (make them acceptable) in the political system. It cannot enforce a policy that is unacceptable to the people it serves and retain power. Thus, schoolmen must continually seek public affirmation of operating policies. The submission of proposals to the electorate of the school district is an illustration of this point. For a detailed description of a school election, see Chapter 7.

The Power Structure

In every community, there must be a structure or system for making decisions concerning community living, for executing policies, and for maintaining the system. Otherwise, the community will disintegrate into disorder and death. Protest groups that complain about the exercise of power by a "power structure" are themselves a part of the structure. They exercise power in the total system by using demonstrations, boycotts, and other techniques. The political system is maintained by power, just as the tiny atom is held together by power. The typical elementary school is a system held together by the exercise of power by the board of education, administrators, teachers, students, parents, and other school personnel. The exercise of power is a legitimate and necessary element in the social order.

The power structure of the community is the systematic, relative distribution of social power among the citizens in determining the kind of community they want and the kind of institutional arrangements that will best serve them. The exercise of power by citizens is not equal; there is an unequal distribution of influence in the system.

Each school district encompasses an area in which an "establishment" or "establishments" decide whether a factory can be built in a certain location, whether school bonds should be floated for new construction, and other civic questions. Decisions in the schools are inextricably tied to massive economic and social decisions not under the direct control of the board of education.

Differing Factors in Power Structures

What is the nature of the power structures within which school systems operate? Within recent years scholars have done extensive research on the power structures of local governments. This body of knowledge has provided some very useful concepts of the power structures of school districts. Schoolmen need no longer accept idealized textbook beliefs about the nature of the political power structure.

Observers of political behavior in the numerous local forms of government throughout a state are impressed by their dissimilarities. Some are stable; others engage in great conflicts. The decisionmaking process in some communities is undemocratic; many are controlled by elite groups. There are so many variables in community political

systems that exact duplication of power structures is improbable within any given state. Some of the elements that differentiate communities are described below.

Influentials of Power Structures

All political systems have leaders who wield a disproportionate amount of power in elections. They are referred to as influentials. The characteristics of influentials vary greatly among power structures. In some school districts, most influentials are native born, whereas in other districts most have moved there from other areas of the country. Variation exists, too, in the influentials' sources of power and the extent of progressiveness they exhibit. The school leader cannot assume blindly that elected public officials are the most powerful men in the school district. Businessmen and professionals who do not hold elective office may wield more power in some communities than public officials. The occupations, backgrounds, beliefs, attitudes, and opinions of the influentials vary widely in different school districts. Generalizing about the makeup of the influentials of a power system, in the absence of empirical data, is therefore foolhardy. School officials must become knowledgeable about the political leaders in their district through direct study.

The influentials, through personal influence with their followers in the school district, mold the opinions of voters concerning the acceptability of educational proposals. The influentials also maintain significant channels of communication and influence with state and national leaders and have resources (e.g., wealth, mass media access, public position, and ties of friendship, kinship, or business relations) that can be used to marshal support for opposition to school proposals submitted to the electorate.

Citizen Participation

School district power structures also vary greatly in the extent and effectiveness of citizen participation in school elections. Variations can be easily demonstrated by comparing the voter turnout in different local governments. Yet voting is the lowest form of sharing in government, since it takes very little time. The more time-consuming forms of engagement (e.g., making speeches, holding public office, canvassing voters, attending meetings, preparing registration lists) are

considered by most authorities to be higher, more effective forms of involvement than the act of voting. The higher forms of participation in school and civic affairs are practically nonexistent in many school districts, while in many others they are characteristic behavior. In "elite-run" power structures, involvement is typically low, whereas it is high and functional in a system of democratic pluralism. These types of power structures are defined and discussed later in this chapter.

The extent to which citizens take part in school affairs influences the outcome of school elections. For example, ineffective citizen participation in school affairs results in lack of reliable information concerning the educational needs of the community. Low public participation also results in an elitism, under which school officials may be subject to the arbitrary whims of a few influentials in the power structure. Education leaders can greatly change the vote in school elections by increasing or discouraging voter turnout, of the entire population or of certain areas of the population.

Norms of the Power Structure

The norms of behavior differ markedly among the local political systems. A norm may be simply defined as the behavior that a group expects of its members. Persons who violate the critical norms of a group are reprimanded (e.g., denied leadership in the group or expelled from the group). The leaders and followers of all political systems have come to accept sets of norms through many years of interaction. Different groups of leaders in the system may well hold different sets of norms, especially if the system is characterized by regime conflicts.

There are numerous illustrations of these norms. For example, in one power structure analyzed by the authors, leaders were expected to be of service to the community, exhibit temperance in their personal habits, and promote harmony as opposed to conflict. Every political system has behavioral norms defining how a leader should use his influence to get things done. Attempting political action in ignorance of the political system's norms is irresponsible leadership. Many school proposals have failed to be accepted in the political system because the leaders for the proposal violated critical norms.

For example, in the power structure of a certain school district, leaders were expected to communicate proposals for informal con-

sideration by the influentials before their formal consideration. The schoolmen ignored this expectation and announced their intention to seek public endorsement of a $30,000,000 bond issue for school construction. This action "hurt the feelings" of several community influentials, who then expressed opposition to the proposal. The educators reacted by attempting to ridicule these opposing influentials publicly, but this violated still another cherished norm in the power structure. These "blunders" led to other mistakes and widespread opposition. The proposal was resoundingly defeated.

Civic Beliefs of Leaders

The beliefs of leaders and followers in the power structure also produce a difference among school districts. This has been documented by examining the extent of civic liberalism among voters, educators, and power-wielders. The Florida Scale of Civic Beliefs indicated considerable variation among 24 school districts in four states.[1] The leader-follower structures of some school districts support conservative, states-rights beliefs; in other districts the leaders and followers support federal social welfare programs.

Political campaigns should be designed to influence the political opinions of leaders in the power structure. One outstanding educator known by the authors advises teachers to encourage politicians to speak about needed school improvements. He contends that if a person speaks about a proposal several times, he begins to believe what he says. There is some truth to this advice. We live in a world of semantics in which much of our experience is through words. The use of words tends to result in the use of thoughts which, in turn, results in action somewhat consistent with the thoughts and words.

If educators can influence the opinions of leaders in the power structure concerning the schools, this will have a tremendous effect on school elections.

Formal and Informal Groups

Although all political systems have many subsystems (interconnecting parts) consisting of organized (formal) and informal groups, the nature of these groups varies greatly. The informal groups are more difficult to learn about than the formal groups since they do not have the constitutions, elected or appointed officers, member-

ship lists, and official meetings that characterize organizations. Nevertheless, they have a definite social structure, norms, communication system, and leadership hierarchy, and they will use their power collectively for certain common goals. The typical faculty clique in a high school is an example of a fairly simple informal group and the sprawling political clique in a power structure exemplifies a more complex one.

Informal groups of the power structure are excellent sources for the exercise of personal influence in school elections. The use of "whisper campaigns" among members of these groups to influence school proposals is one example; for others, see Chapter 3.

There are so many different organizations (formal groups), performing myriad activities in the political system, that classification is difficult but probably only a few of these groups (and perhaps, in some cases, none) have importance in a given political activity. Therefore, educational leaders must assess the propensity of organized groups to participate in educational elections. An organization's political significance is also proportional to the extent that its membership is made up of community influentials. School leaders must recognize, however, that all organizations are potentially useful to those directing political activity. Even an organization with no political influence, because it is a center of social interaction for its members, provides impact on and reinforcement for the political opinions of its members. Organizations also provide convenient audiences for speakers, films, and other forms of propaganda.

The political parties are, of course, well-known organizations in partisan campaigns. However, studies of political activity do not indicate that many community party officials are very influential.[2] They tend to perform maintenance leadership activities rather than opinion leadership. Little empirical evidence is available concerning the functions of political parties in nonpartisan school elections. Nevertheless, school leaders should study the leadership hierarchies in political parties in the school district.

Within recent years the leaders of protest groups have plunged schoolmen into raw political activity. These groups are particularly important in ghetto areas of cities where the most unstable groups of city power structures reside. The rapidly changing leadership patterns in these areas of great structural fluidity complicate decisionmaking.

The school administrator must discover the formal and informal groups that are the subsystems of the total power structure, based on

his firsthand observation. This knowledge may be imperative in organizing and directing political activity in school elections. For instance, in many school districts parent-teacher organizations have provided the nucleus of personnel for carrying out political activities for school projects.

The Communication System

The interaction structure of the power system must be studied. What are the communication networks in the system? Is there more transmission of information downward or upward in the governing process? Who are the key communicators? Power structures are characterized by operative channels of interchange within the horizontal levels of the system. Political leaders have contact with leaders of ethnic groups, families, and other formal and informal groups. Very little activity of political significance escapes the attention of a strong, well-organized power group. For example, a city political machine, organized down to the ward and block level, usually has fast and impressive communication mechanisms.

Establishing functional means of interchange with significant formal and informal subsystems has not been the forte of school administrators. School principals should be encouraged to establish and maintain contact with the opinion leaders in their attendance area. The superintendent of schools and other key persons of the central administrative staff should consciously develop and use several channels in interacting with the influentials of the political system.

In 1967, one of the authors directed a power study in a local district. During the study he became interested in determining how often educators had talked personally about schools with the influentials of the power structure. What he found was not encouraging: A preponderance of the influentials reported that no professional school leader had attempted to talk personally with them about the schools in over 15 years.

By contrast, another school superintendent established a very operative communication network with influentials and leaders in his school district. Over a period of years the superintendent had developed close personal acquaintance with persons living and working in all parts of the district who held key positions in the political system's communication network. The superintendent had an informal agreement with these persons that (1) they would report to him

immediately any adverse conversation about the schools that they thought could be significant, (2) they would spend specified periods of time, at his request, listening to and judging public opinion on specific educational problems or issues, and (3) they would help him transmit to the public certain key ideas concerning educational developments.

This system proved to be an excellent source of feedback to the superintendent. Through this continuing communication net he was able to know what of significance was going on in the total power structure of the district. The authors are not advocating this approach, however, because it has some obvious limitations. For example, complete dependence on personal sources could in time produce slanted feedback. A scientifically based poll, such as those discussed in Chapter 4, should provide more objectively accurate feedback. Nevertheless, the example provides a commendable illustration of how a schoolman established useful means of interchange with leaders in the power structure. Operative channels of communication provide invaluable means for convincing influentials and citizens in school election campaigns and for providing significant feedback concerning community reception to the schools.

Understanding the Total System

The basic concepts discussed above illustrate some of the important elements in the total power system that school leaders should understand as a basis for initiating political action. It is most important, however, that school leaders understand how the dynamics of behavior affect the total power structure; how the system may be influenced through political activity; and how to predict accurately the consequences of alternative strategies for school elections. This understanding can be achieved only by studying the power structure of the particular school district.

Types of Power Structures

Writers have tried, with some success, to fit the power structures of local government into classification systems which school executives may find useful in studying their districts. Some types of power structures are discussed below.

Monopolistic Systems

The existence of monopolistic, or monolithic, power structures has been revealed in numerous case studies. These structures take many forms. Some are "political machines." Others are ruled by a singular structure of influentials who do not hold elective public office. There are still a few "one industry" towns in which politics is dominated by the company owners. Some rural communities are governed by groups of large landowners. The typical controlled community is run by a single group of influentials composed of a mixture of business-men, professionals, politicians, and other occupational interests.

In the monopolistic power structure, a surprisingly small number of influentials dictates major policies. In 1953, Hunter shocked the academic community with his finding that a city of 500,000 persons was run by a handful of powerful men in the economic sector.[3] The more powerful of these men did not even hold elective public office.

The Hunter study was followed by revelations in numerous studies that, although a few top influentials of a political system may indeed dominate decisions, this dominance may not be complete. Opposition may be exercised in issues that provoke sufficient interest, but the opposition is typically sporadic and does not continue through two consecutive elections in an organized fashion.

One of the characteristics of monopolistic systems is the absence of "regime" conflicts in which there are heated, fairly evenly matched confrontations on issues dealing with "the kind of community we want." If there are no conflicts about the community's emphasis on tourism, industry, trade, or other economic bases, a ruling power elite group with a high degree of agreement is possible, and conflicts are restricted to procedural questions, such as who goes to what school, the teaching of reading, and contractual negotiations.

In a monopolistic system, viable citizen and group involvement in such decisions as building civic auditoriums, establishing industrial parks, controlling planning and zoning activities, electing school board members, and providing recreational activities is largely nonex-istent. To what extent are the collective views of citizens represented in governance of the district? In monopolistic systems citizen repre-sentation is minimized through a tradition of apathy, fear of sanc-tions, lack of organization, and other factors.

Furthermore, not all persons who have power resources use them. For example, although wealth or the control of wealth can be readily

converted to political power, not all the wealthy men in a school district can be assumed to be influentials. Many wealthy persons choose not to use this resource for the accumulation of political power. The managers of absentee-owned corporations may or may not be active in the power structure. Teachers traditionally did not engage in political activities. Thousands of citizens are apathetic and, consequently, exert little political power. These various unused sources of power are referred to as latent centers of power, and they usually abound in a monopolistic power structure. In fact, their activation can be a strategy used to influence monopolistic systems, although excessive use of revolutionary strategies is not without political consequences to the organizers.

Multigroup Noncompetitive Structures

Most experienced school administrators have observed school districts in which most of the influentials and their followers have reached a high degree of agreement about the kind of community they want. To illustrate, the influentials of one school district known to the authors generally agree that they want to keep the area free of "smelly" industries, overcommercialized tourism, and other developments that would destroy the community's image as a nice, middle class, residential area. Most of the influentials have lived there all of their lives and consider the schools, as they often express it in their conversation, "the best schools in the state." There are no demands to change the basic nature of schooling.

Within this total power system, characterized by consensus on basic community policy, there are, however, rival groups interested in furthering their economic advantage. Leaders of these groups do not hold critically different beliefs about the nature of good schools and how they should be administered, but there is rivalry between these power blocs concerning the acquisition of contracts and fees. The leaders often fight over such things as the location of consolidated schools, the awarding of contracts for public services or building contracts, and the handling of insurance.

This type of power system, called the multigroup noncompetitive structure, is often typified by the rural school district serving several incorporated towns. Each of the towns has a power group that has an "our town" identification. The leaders of these towns enter into rivalry concerning the location of consolidated schools, hospitals,

federal highways, factories, or other developments perceived to be of economic advantage. Yet, the influentials and followers agree about the kind of community they want and the nature of schools that can best serve that community. There is political consensus among the influentials and their followers concerning the nature of government at the local, state, and national levels.

Competitive Elite Systems

The reader is no doubt familiar with school districts in which there is extreme competition concerning the style of community living. There are two or more powerful groups engaged in regime conflicts characterized by an intense power struggle over "what kind of town ours shall be." The political atmosphere is electrified by questions of planning and zoning, hospitalization, property assessment, education, industrialism, tourism, sewage treatment, and public health. Groups struggle bitterly over elections of officials to public office. Yet there is insufficient citizen participation, and most of the involvement comes from the influentials of elite groups.

Competitive elite systems are characterized by struggles between power blocs. The influentials engaged in these struggles have conflicting beliefs about the kind of community desired. The structure falls short of a democratic pluralism (described below) in several respects. Citizen engagement in policy making is neither widespread nor functional. Organized interest groups are more the captives of informal power blocs than they are the basis of citizen participation. The power blocs tend to have a generalized interest in the policies of all institutional sectors as opposed to the specialized leadership activity of segmented pluralisms. The structure is more open to the emergence of new leaders, however, than monopolistic or multigroup noncompetitive structures. It is tending toward but has not achieved the status of a mature democratic system.

The Democratic Pluralism

The political systems of many school districts have been described as democratic pluralisms. A democratic pluralism is characterized by several (often many) competing bases of power. Various organized interest groups are important centers of power in civic decisions and the influence of informal general power blocs is minimized. The

system is open to the emergence of new persons and groups to positions of influence. The influentials tend to change as the issues and decisions change. The persons who influence a decision in community health may be different from those who influence an educational decision. Citizens participate effectively in public policy through membership in influential organizations and through viable activity in the election of public officials. The decisionmaking process is consistent with democratic ideals.

Pluralism is the most democratic of all power systems discussed above and it is probably the most open to the emergence of leadership influence. Thus, a school superintendent who is new to a community could probably achieve more power (influence) using less time and effort in a pluralistic than in a monopolistic power structure. There are fewer latent power centers in the pluralism than in the typical monopolistic system. Most centers of power are fully politicized. Elected and appointed public officials hold higher power status in a pluralistic structure than in a monopolistic structure dominated by economic and political elites.

Structures of Suburban School Districts

Many persons have held the view that the power structure of "bedroom" suburban communities is different from that of the typical city or rural school district. It is felt that suburban communities do not actually develop a power structure because the population is changing and otherwise unstable. Is this a valid concept of suburban communities?

Minar investigated in depth the governing processes of several suburban school districts near Chicago.[4] The findings from his study serve as a warning to those who attempt to generalize about power in the absence of empirical data. For example, one school district had a low-conflict, orderly, highly structured system of governance. Its system acted as a powerful conflict-suppressant. Another of the districts studied had a high-conflict system. Board meetings were long and chaotic, and the organizational structure of the schools appeared haphazard. Yet the socioeconomic characteristics of these two districts were very similar. In summary, Minar's analysis gave no general support to the idea that the political systems of suburban school districts are radically different from those of other districts or that all suburban districts are alike.

The authors certainly agree that some suburban school districts undergo periods in which power exchanges are so swift that the power structure defies description. Also, many suburban school districts experience periods of such rapid growth and population change that the political system is very open, pliable, and changing. There are, perhaps, some districts in which a sense of powerlessness seems momentarily present. But a semblance of organization and of the decisionmaking mechanisms still exists.

In conducting elections in disorganized communities, the school leaders must help the district develop a definable power structure in so far as public education is concerned. For example, solutions to problems in ghetto communities marked by tumult are impossible until an identifiable power structure emerges. Therefore, school leaders may, in fact, need to help establish or, at least, further develop the school district's power structure in order to conduct successful school elections. This is quite a shift from the educator's traditional view that power is evil and should be opposed.

If schoolmen face a "mushy," fluctuating political system in which leadership changes rapidly, a significant part of the strategy for school elections is to build a stable power structure for the schools. Education leaders will need to identify persons throughout the district who will work for better schools and who have some community or neighborhood influence. They should enlist the services of these persons in helping to promote positive attitudes about school improvement proposals and in providing leadership in school elections.

Dynamics of Power Structures

School officials should not plan elections in ignorance of the dynamics of the power structure. The behavior of the structure will greatly influence the outcome of elections. Election campaigns do not deal with an amorphous mass of citizens who are equal in their ability to make ideas acceptable. Except for the minority of school districts going through periods of disorganization or development, the district in which schoolmen will be exercising leadership will be a highly structured, complex power system, with hierarchies (or a hierarchy) of leadership.

Some of the influentials in the hierarchies hold enormous power resources to influence elections; these men are phenomenally more

influential than the man-on-the-street. If a given influential surmises that the schools need additional millage, his followers will tend to view a school proposal to increase millage positively, or at least they will not rush to oppose it. If the influential voices disapproval, his following is going to have some doubt about the wisdom of a proposal to increase the taxes. Whether the power structure is monopolistic, pluralistic, or another type, the actions of influentials can assist in the acceptance or rejection of educational proposals.

Ranking below the top influentials of the power structure is an odd assortment of power-wielders, grassroots leaders, elected officials, minor political leaders, and persons performing various functions to maintain the system. Some of the grassroots leaders are 100 percent politicians, commonly referred to by a host of role-differentiating names such as henchmen, lackeys, wardheelers, petty politicians, legmen, and party men. These leaders have specialized abilities to motivate other men toward the general goals of their power group. For example, the wardheeler of a city political machine specializes in moving men to action according to directions predetermined by influentials in the party. The elected official often uses his authority to the advantage of certain policies. Those in charge of the mass media can mount "campaigns" for causes considered important by certain political leaders.

The minor political leaders perform essential functions in election campaigns. They have made a livelihood of politics and have close personal contact with many constituents. Since they are thoroughly familiar with the realities of political behavior, they serve as excellent organizers at the grassroots level, and the more influential minor politicians are significant information links. Although these minor leaders are not the policymakers of power groups, they can influence the thinking of those who decide goals and strategies. Therefore, school leaders should not discount their importance. Their influence in an election can be felt in all precincts, wards, villages, and neighborhoods of a school district.

Communication among the influentials, leaders, followers, and supporters of a power bloc is very effective. Few significant developments go unnoticed and unreported. Opposing groups keep general surveillance of each other's activities.

The members of a power group are held together by many different kinds of ties. Many of them have interlocking business ties. Competing banks may serve as the financial institutional ties of compet-

ing power groups. Strong friendship ties are developed, and family ties become very important among the leaders and followers of many power structures. Through years of interaction and exchange of ideas, the leaders and their followers find satisfaction in working toward a certain ideal of community living.

Interaction among influentials, leaders, and followers of a power group are frequent and functional. For example, many of the influentials may belong to the same country club or attend the same church. They give a great deal of thought to community living and frequently discuss business and social conditions. In communities that have fairly stable populations this exchange of ideas results in the development of norms and ideals about community living. The leaders have very definite concepts about what kind of a community they want, what kind of schools will serve the community, and how they expect school superintendents, principals, and teachers to behave.

The process of developing norms about community living (and education) is of critical importance to educators planning long range developments. School leaders must be a part of this dynamic process. Rather than attempting to insulate themselves from the dynamics of power, educators must be represented in the daily discussions of "what kind of town we want." By exercising their power in this process, they can establish baseline concepts in the interest of quality schools that will support a series of successful school elections for years to come.

The influence of power-wielders does not stop at the boundaries of school districts. These men may have close ties with state and national political leaders. They may address the governor, senators, and other high-ranking officials by their first names. These ties provide a means for bringing outside resources to bear on election campaigns in school districts — a fact never to be overlooked by school officials. However, state politics, like politics in many local governments, is usually competitive. Therefore, local leaders will not control all the state-level resources that may be useful in state and local campaigns. Also, unwise use of outside resources may create backlashes in local elections. The possibility of local resentment of "outsider" manipulation helps to modify the open use of state power in campaigns of strictly local concern, although state power may be used covertly.

State and national leaders control some important resources, such as widespread patronage activity. Local and state leaders hold politi-

cal obligations (IOU's) from each other, which they "cash in" to obtain action on proposals in which they are interested. Thus, significant decisions in local school districts may involve state influentials.

Closed Political Systems

The power structures of many communities are characterized more by their closedness than by their openness. Communities with stable populations and slow business development often become closed to inputs from outside the system. Many monopolistic and multigroup noncompetitive power structures exhibit this characteristic and do not allow the emergence of new leadership having ideas in competition with the prevailing norms. Winning an election over the opposition of an active power structure with a high degree of closure is very difficult, unless power in the structure is redistributed.

Retaining control over election campaigns in a closed power system is a tenuous matter. The behavior of the top influentials is not necessarily dependent upon public thinking. Effective citizen involvement in governance is low. The behavior of large numbers of latent power centers is unpredictable. Will these centers become involved in the school election? Will some of them participate? What percentage of the apathetic citizenry will decide to contribute leadership and vote in the campaign? If all the citizens and power groups of a school district were fully politicized (100 percent participative) and outside influences on the district were stabilized, the outcome of school elections could be accurately predicted. This accuracy is not possible in school districts in which massive power interests are involved in local campaigns only sporadically. Thus, active involvement should be encouraged and fostered.

Educators may use several approaches in monopolistic power structures to win elections. They may try to convince the influentials to support school improvement proposals before taking official action calling for an election. This has been successful in many school districts. On the other hand, some school leaders have not been able to convince the influentials that certain proposals were desirable. If the educational leaders find much opposition to a proposal among the influentials of a monopolistic power structure, they still have some options, however. They can delay elections until they win more support among the influentials or they can mobilize latent groups of power in the structure and conduct a grassroots campaign, to defeat

the influentials and their followers. These alternatives have been used successfully in different school districts. The choice of an approach should be based on a careful study of the political situation, with special attention to the consequences of political activity.

Open Political Systems

Many political systems are noted for their openness. Unlike the closed system, the open system uses inputs from outside itself as a basis for redefining goals and changing direction. The processes of governance are characterized by a greater degree of citizen involvement, especially in pluralistic systems. The system is open to the emergence of new leaders and new power groups, and there is competition among ideas about community living. No group or coalition of groups has a hold on the nature of the educational system. Competitive elite and pluralistic power structures are open systems.

Mounting winning elections in power structures characterized by openness calls for different strategies than those needed for closed political systems. For example, in the pluralistic community the influentials tend to change as community issues change. The group of influentials working to change planning and zoning policies will not usually participate in a decision to add three mills to the school budget. The influentials interested in a school construction program may not take part in significant curriculum decisions. Therefore, in planning campaign strategies for school elections, educators must first identify the influentials most interested in the proposal being submitted to the electorate.

The traditional grassroots approach is necessary in school elections regardless of the type of power structure. However, it is much more effective in power structures having openness than in closed systems. Since the power groups of a democratic pluralism are active, there is less chance of miscalculations of an election outcome because of sporadic (and unexpected) participation of latent centers of power. Hence, the results of public opinion polls are more reliable in a pluralism (assuming that outside influences remain normal), and the citizens should be responsive to a variety of information campaigns by school leaders concerning school conditions.

The competitive elite structure presents quite a different problem for political activity than the pluralism. Citizen involvement in governance is not as extensive in competitive elite power structures. The

struggle for power over decisions is between elite-controlled power groups. Very sharp differences in opinion about educational policies are likely to be present. Consequently, the political activities of educators may be focused on building agreement and seeking compromises between the influentials of warring groups. Otherwise, education leaders may needlessly sacrifice school development by allowing the schools to become the object of a community power struggle in which concern for the welfare of students is lost. Education leaders must establish processes that facilitate interaction between the influentials and followers of opposing power groups. The object, of course, is to encourage commitments to quality schools from otherwise dissident groups of influentials.

Techniques that maximize cooperative planning should be emphasized when educators are dealing with a competitive elite structure. Much energy should be invested in seeing that the key influentials of competing groups have the opportunity to participate in the planning process. These influentials need to be fully informed of the educational goals. All planning activity is aimed to build agreements concerning educational policies, which will decrease the possibility of a power struggle among the groups in school improvement elections.

If all efforts fail to bring agreement on educational policies among the influentials of a competitive elite structure, educators may face a tragic power struggle. If the struggle is simply a "spillover" from regime conflicts in other institutional sectors of the community, and true regime conflict over the schools is not present, the educator may still be able to effect reasonable compromise and spare disruptive conflict in the schools. If regime conflict concerning the kind of schools desired is present, however, schoolmen will probably be forced to make alignments and join in the struggle. Let us suppose, for example, that the power struggle involves ultraconservative versus moderate positions concerning the nature of the instructional program and the size of the school budget. The authors do not believe that the school children will be served in this instance by submissive opportunism from the educational leaders. They must take positions in such struggles and use all their political knowledge to marshal political power for their views. School elections in such circumstances are the means by which regime conflicts are resolved.

Techniques for Researching the Power Structure

Two techniques have been widely used by scholars in the study of community power structures. Neither method can be used by the school administrator in the way that it is employed by "outside" researchers. If the practicing administrator attempted the direct use of either method, not only could he not obtain the cooperation of those he attempted to interview, but in all probability he would also jeopardize his position. Nevertheless, through knowledge of these techniques the educator may be able to apply the required steps informally.

Reputational Technique

Hunter used the reputational technique in his study of Atlanta, Georgia.[5] The technique generally encompasses four steps. First, persons who are at the center of community activities are asked to provide lists of persons of prominence in the institutional sectors of the community (economics, government, education, religion, etc.) and persons of wealth and social prominence. These lists may be obtained from such sources as the community council, the League of Women Voters, the chamber of commerce, newspaper editors, and persons known to be active in the civic and social life of the community.

The second step is to ask a panel of knowledgeable persons to select from the lists those persons who, in their opinion, are most influential. A final list is compiled, consisting of those persons whom the panel of judges, acting independently, agree are the most prominent leaders on the list.

The third step is to conduct in-depth interviews with these listed prominent persons. Forty or more interviews, of from two to six hours or more, may be required. The leaders are asked to provide information about (1) issues, problems, and decisions in the community, (2) their participation in these issues, problems, and decisions, (3) the participation of other leaders, (4) friendship ties with other leaders in the community, (5) business ties, (6) their estimate of the relative influence of other prominent leaders, (7) kinship patterns, (8) information about power groups, and (9) other information useful in understanding the dynamics of the power structure. During these interviews other prominent leaders will be added to the list of persons to be interviewed.

The final step is to organize and interpret the massive amount of data collected to provide a description of the power structure in the community.

Decision Analysis Technique

In his study of New Haven, Connecticut, Dahl used a decision analysis technique.[6] The first step is to select several decision areas (e.g., education, community health, business, urban renewal, planning and zoning) and ask persons representative of these areas to identify the most significant decisions made in their areas within recent years.

The second step is to obtain as much information as possible about the decisions identified. Data are obtained from various documents, newspapers, direct observation, and interviews. Extensive, in-depth interviews are conducted with persons known to have participated in the decisions selected for analysis. From intensive study of the decisions and those furnishing leadership in initiating and making them, the research team attempts to reconstruct the power dynamics of each decision. Who initiated action in each decision? Who controlled the decision outcome? How did these persons exercise power in the decision? Who was charged with implementing the decision? What were the patterns of citizen participation?

The final step is to describe the nature of the power structure as indicated by the data on the decisions in different areas.

Combining Research Techniques

For several years considerable difference of opinion existed among authorities concerning the advantages and disadvantages of the two techniques. Some studies have demonstrated that the techniques provide similar findings on the exercise of power in the community, particularly in identifying those in the most powerful categories. Presthus has suggested that the reputational and decision analysis techniques may be combined to give a more completely accurate description of the power structure than when only one technique is used.[7] The authors concur with this view.

Nevertheless, as stated earlier, the practicing school administrator or teacher cannot use either of these techniques or a combination of them in a formal manner. Imagine, for example, what might transpire

in the community if the superintendent of schools began formal interviews with influentials asking them for all kinds of personal information, e.g., how they got things done in the community, and their feelings about the behavior of other leaders. He would be lucky if he avoided being abruptly dismissed from his position. Educators will have to apply the steps in these techniques in an informal way, just as outstanding schoolmen have always done.

Applying Research Techniques in a School District

School leaders studying the power structure of their own districts may use some of the following practical suggestions and alternative steps. Studying the power structure is not an avocation of the superintendent of schools and his colleagues, but a serious part of the modern school leader's job. Progressive changes in the public schools may well depend on the scholarship of schoolmen in understanding the political system of their school districts.

Step One: Background Study

The first important step is taken when the school leader accepts the idea that a uniquely shaped power structure exists in his school district and attempts to define it empirically. In preparation for this task, educational leaders should read books and published research reports containing studies of power structure. (See the suggested readings at the end of this chapter.) Courses, workshops, and conferences on the politics of education are also available. From these materials and activities the leader will broaden his perspective of political systems as a basis for better understanding his own school district.

Step Two: Learning the Problems, Issues, and Decisions

The authors suggest that schoolmen initiate get-acquainted, informal discussions with leaders in important sectors of the school district. The persons to be contacted will vary according to the socioeconomic characteristics of the district, but may include (1) the executive secretary or president of the chamber of commerce, (2) well-known politicians, (3) prominent attorneys, (4) prominent physicians, (5) prominent bankers, (6) leaders in women's clubs and

social activities, (7) labor union leaders, (8) clergymen, (9) chairmen of executive committees of Republican and Democratic parties, (10) the publisher or editor of the local newspaper, (11) the manager of the local television or radio station, (12) a farm agent or prominent farmer, and (13) leaders of influential ethnic and racial groups in the school district.

The authors are not suggesting that the school leaders seek formal interviews with these persons. If educators are active in civic affairs they will find opportunities to talk extensively with many of these persons. For example, the school superintendent may sit with the president of the bank at a civic club or engage in conversation with the manager of the television station before appearing on a school-related TV broadcast.

The first step in talking with these persons is to get them to discuss the problems, issues, and decisions important to them. Schoolmen should make an effort to understand fully the issues and decisions that have made or are making the greatest impact on the thinking of these persons. As these concerns and interests are discussed, educators should make mental notes of the persons frequently mentioned in connection with the issues, problems, or decisions. They should encourage discussion that indicates who are the most influential persons in the community, according to these informants. This is not difficult. Most people enjoy talking about their community and who is important in it.

Step Three: Piecing Together Conversations and Documents

The school leader can learn a great deal about the power structure through these conversations. He should record the names of all persons mentioned as prominent, and he should be especially cognizant of the relationships between them. People commonly make statements such as "Herb Bennett is in the First Bank crowd," "Robert Finley is Jimmy Bolles' son-in-law," or "Skip Burns is the governor's man in Springlake." Every person with whom the school leader talks may give him a piece of information that fits together with other pieces like a puzzle.

Another important source of information about the community power structure is documents. The boards of directors of financial institutions, for example, are usually published. The names of leaders of community groups may be easily obtained from the chamber of

commerce or other associations. The membership lists of some organizations might be sought. Newspapers should be read with a view to identifying community leaders. The names of prominent public officials are, of course, readily available.

Step Four: Recording and Compiling Information

While carrying out steps two and three, the school leader should record all information pertinent to understanding the power structure. This is very important, since few persons are able to organize mentally and recall all politically significant information. Documentary material and newspaper clippings should also be filed and continually updated and evaluated.

In addition to gathering information on the power dynamics of the school district, the educators should marshal resources for exercising power within that structure. The names of persons who express particular interest in working for better schools should be noted. They will serve as a reservoir of support in school election campaigns. Likewise, notation should be made of persons who express predispositions to oppose school proposals. Immediate plans should be made to work with these persons, encourage them to participate in school affairs, and provide information to them concerning educational needs in the community.

Step Five: Direct Observation and Participation in Community Activities

"Birdwatching" is an excellent means of gathering information about the power structure. Schoolmen should make it their business to observe power behavior directly. They should concentrate attention on significant decisionmaking activities and look beneath the public manifestations of leadership activities in the decision. Who were the most influential citizens in initiation of the decisionmaking activity? Who exerted influence behind the scenes? Who were the legmen, playing minor political roles in the decision? What groups of leaders were involved? Was there regime-like competition in the decisionmaking process? To what extent did citizens participate in the process? What attitudes and beliefs did the influentials express?

Observations of political activities are most fruitful when the schoolmen are testing ideas about the type of power structure they

believe exists. This prevents meaningless random observations. For example, if the educator believes that a pluralistic power structure exists, he can look for certain clues. Are there different groups of leaders for different issue areas in the community? How extensive is citizen participation in decisions?

In order to carry out "birdwatching" in the analysis of power, active participation in civic activities in the community is necessary. From his observation of and participation in community affairs, the schoolman builds a satisfactory description of the power dynamics of the school district.

Thoughtful engagement in political activities by school leaders will provide a "gut-level" conceptualization of the power structure. In other words, the school leader will learn much about politics by attempting to influence the system. In conducting his first election in the district, the schoolman may or may not be successful, but regardless of the outcome, the activity should make him wiser about the power structure. He should use his experience in the unsuccessful campaign as one of the bases for better understanding politics in his school district.

Success in Study of the Power Structure

The authors know of a case in which study of the power structure was the key to success for the school superintendent of a medium-sized school district. Before his appointment as superintendent of the district, two referenda for a school building program had been decisively defeated, most recently by a 2 to 1 majority.

The new school superintendent was employed by the board of education with the understanding that his primary task was to seek public acceptance of a building program. He used some of the approaches discussed above to make a study of the power structure. Within an 18-month period he provided the leadership necessary to reverse the two previous election results and pass a school bonding proposal by a 2 to 1 vote. The authors believe that this is an outstanding accomplishment.

The superintendent became personally absorbed in studying the dynamics of power as exercised in decisions. The main technique he used was to have private luncheons with prominent persons in the community, at which he talked about development of the schools and learned the names of other prominent leaders in the community.

As these names were mentioned, the superintendent made "mental notes" of each and later wrote them down for permanent reference and analysis. He also listened for information about the relationships between these leaders. Furthermore, he was alert to any information that would help him conceptualize the shape of power in the school district.

By concentrating attention on the dynamics of power through many conversations with many persons, the school superintendent, within a few months, had what he thought was a complete picture of the power structure. He deliberately planned his total educational improvement strategy to mesh with and to be most effective in the dynamics of this structure.

In the first place, he was able to achieve high participation of the influentials in studying educational needs. This was possible because he knew who they were and had established personal relationships with each. Secondly, his strategy involved taking the proposal through these leaders to the people. Citizens were encouraged to participate in planning activities and, because of the interest of their leaders, many did. As a result, controversy was very low in the election campaign, whereas it had been tumultuous in the prevous elections. This strategy was superbly effective in improving education.

This school superintendent proved that, with knowledge of the literature and previous research experience in the study of power structure, the practicing school administrator can accurately conceptualize the political system. His personal experience was followed by a carefully directed study of the school district power structure by a university group. When the university results were compared with his results, he was in error on only one fact: He had failed to realize that he himself had achieved a high position of power in the system. This, the authors believe, is another significant accomplishment. It proves that educators can become powerful in political systems within a short period of time by providing modern leadership for modern conditions. Through this position of leadership they have much greater opportunity to assure quality education for children than they have from a position of powerlessness.

As a final point, this case demonstrates that well-planned and well-led campaigns can change the opinions of voters. Educators can indeed work with the board of education and other community leaders to legitimize educational ideas. If it is possible to change the vote on a bonding proposal from a 2 to 1 defeat to a 2 to 1 victory in a

tough-minded community, few educational needs should be impossible to legitimize.

Use of Studies Conducted by External Groups

School officials may feel the need to compare their own observations with studies conducted by external study groups. For example, arrangements could be made with university personnel to bring in a team to make a community study. The professional survey should include community analyses from which impressions of the power structure may be forthcoming. For obvious reasons, some information about community leadership will not be included in the formal survey report, but a study by outsiders will strengthen the objectivity of perceptions formed from educators' own studies of power.

In one case, comparison of the results of a study by the school superintendent and an independent in-depth study conducted by university students indicated that, in most respects, the findings were comparable. However, the superintendent reported that the data collected by the students helped him understand better certain aspects of power he had previously overlooked.

Testing the Accuracy of Knowledge of the Structure

How can a school leader determine that he has enough information to conceptualize the dynamics of the political system correctly? There are several tests, in addition to comparing his findings with those of an external study group, as discussed above. One indication may be the realization of a point of saturation where additional information adds nothing new. This is only useful for short periods, however, because power structures are in a continuous process of change.

The most important test point is predictability. When the educator feels that he can predict political behavior in the community, and does so, he has accurately conceptualized the political system. Educators should engage in this process continuously and observe the results of their predictions objectively.

Another test of accuracy is gained by having some idea of what the educator might and should find, from broad reading in the literature. There is no substitute for being generally informed in the politics of education. For example, if a person found that 500 persons were key

influentials in a town of 10,000 population, we might have reason to question his conclusions, because research in similar sized districts leads us to expect from 15 to 40 key influentials. Likewise, if the person found that all of his community influentials were teachers, he would have a very unusual finding. This does not mean that it cannot be true of a school district. (We have emphasized that the power structure for each district is unique in some respects.) However, most studies show that the influentials of school districts include representatives from a variety of occupational interests.

The final test of an educator's ideas is to try them in political activity in the district. Schoolmen will soon learn how well they have conceptualized the power structure when they attempt to conduct a school election. How well did they predict who the influentials in the election would be? Did these persons use the methods expected in supporting or opposing the proposal? What were the sources of the influentials' power in the election? Did the formal and informal groups serve the power-related functions expected? Were schoolmen able to activate latent centers of power in the structure as planned and did this make the difference expected? Success in practice is indeed a very significant test of the accuracy of ideas.

Tailoring Political Strategies to the Power Structure

Too many school officials use standard procedures in running election campaigns regardless of the nature of the power structure in their school districts. This is a futile business and has resulted in many needlessly defeated school proposals.

For example, a certain school district decided to hold a school bond election. When the campaign was well along, opposition emerged. Several persons outside the system were asked to meet and discuss what should be done in light of the opposition. The meeting revealed that the school leaders had not attempted to communicate with and solicit the help of influentials in the power structure. In fact, they demonstrated great ignorance as to who the influentials were. Other weaknesses in their school bond campaigns included very poor organization. The school bond proposal was defeated by less than 50 votes. Two years later, with the active support of influentials in the power structure, the same proposal passed by a 3 to 1 vote, but in the meantime, and until the new facilities were available, the schools were subjected to pitifully overcrowded conditions.

In another case, a school superintendent who had previously served in a stable, upper middle class, suburban school district, was appointed superintendent in a large city, ruled by a well-structured monopolistic power system. In running a school bond referendum in the city, he chose a typical grassroots approach that might have been effective in a democratic pluralism. When warned about the weakness of his strategy in his city, the superintendent replied, "I know how to run bond elections. I have passed many bond election proposals." The referendum failed by more than a 5 to 1 margin.

The point is that school campaigns should be tailored to the kind of political power system the educator is seeking to influence. Perhaps the bond election in the city school system would have failed by the best of strategies; however, running a bond election proposal that lost by a 5 to 1 margin may have been unwise. The energy spent could well have been saved for another more profitable time, when a strategy tailored to the realities of the monopolistic power structure might result in passage of the proposal.

In urging school leaders to tailor political strategy, the authors would like to point out once more that they are not advocating the use of cheap political manipulation in a Machiavellian framework. Instead, we are advocating common sense democracy. Attempting to run a school system without knowing who the influentials are in the community is irresponsible leadership. Modeling a political strategy without knowledge of the dynamics of power of the system sought to be influenced is an unwise use of resources. When school leaders plan election strategies, they are (or are supposed to be) "treating" the political system. Their aim is to influence the system in such a way that it accepts healthy schools.

To illustrate the merit of considering alternative strategies, two extreme cases are described:

In Case A, the power structure of the school district is monopolistic and steeply pyramided toward a few businessmen, politicans, and professionals. These men control powerful resources and have very large followings. In the past their support of school improvement proposals has resulted in widespread public approval. The managers of absentee-owned corporations in the district have taken little interest in political affairs.

Case B involves an upper middle class suburban school district. The power structure resembles the democratic pluralism described earlier in this chapter. Public participation in decisionmaking is high and

effective. The persons identified as influentials tend to change with a change in the issue or decision being considered. The PTA is a very influential group in educational issues.

When we consider how to organize winning millage election campaigns in these very different power structures, we find that the strategy that will be successful in one may fail miserably in the other. For example, complete reliance on a well-organized grassroots approach, without reference to the thoughts of influentials, would probably be successful in Case B. The same strategy runs considerable risk of failure in Case A because too much power is held by key influentials who may oppose the millage. Consequently, the strategy for Case A must include techniques to obtain cooperation of influentials in addition to the usual grassroots campaign.

In both cases, alternative approaches and strategies should be considered and tested conceptually for possible consequences in the political system. For example, suppose that the influentials of Case A steadfastly oppose a needed school improvement project that must be submitted to the electorate. Educators must contemplate the consequences of the following approaches:

(1) attempting to organize latent centers of power (e.g., managers of absentee-owned corporations) and the public to defeat the existing power structure,

(2) bringing pressure from outside sources to bear, to change the opinions of some of the influentials (e.g., the threat of losing the schools' accreditation or eventual loss of economic growth, because of poor schools),

(3) organizing studies of school needs in which key influentials participate and grow in their understanding of school needs (e.g., cooperative school surveys, citizens committees),

(4) acquiescing to the wishes of the influentials until school conditions get bad enough for public pressure to force a change in their opinions,

(5) forgetting about the idea of pressing for school improvement,

(6) considering changes in the school proposal that might make it acceptable to the leaders in the community, and

(7) attempting to bargain with the influentials for their support by promising advantages to them for supporting the proposal.

The authors do not claim to have exhausted all conceivable approaches in the above list. The choices tend to fall into categories. Approach 1 is a revolutionary strategy designed to force a redistribu-

tion of power in the district. Approaches 2 and 3 are evolutionary approaches based on persuasion within the existing power structure. Approaches 4 and 5 refuse responsibility for aggressive leadership for school improvement. Approach 6 is a compromise strategy. Approach 7 is an opportunistic strategy. What are the consequences of these alternative approaches for winning a school election within the power structure of Case A? What are the long range consequences of their use for good governance of schools? Although the authors do not like the idea of using some (particularly Approaches 5 and 7), all have been used in practice.

Schoolmen should be creative in organizing modern campaigns that are effective for the particular districts they serve. An illustrative case study in Chapter 7 shows how educators in one community were able to use information about the power structure to mount a winning strategy.

Leadership in Improving the Political System

School leaders of the future will probably show greater interest in the kinds of power structures that existed in their school districts than did their predecessors. Somehow the quality of education in a school district seems to be conditioned by the maturity of the power system in which the schools function; a healthy school system rarely develops in a "sick" political system. Therefore, schoolmen cannot ignore their civic responsibilities in cooperating with other citizens to develop mature power structures. In school districts verging on anarchy, of course, school leaders are faced with the problem of establishing a stable political system through which schools can operate effectively.

The democratic pluralism may offer a model power structure for educators. Through their cooperative participation and leadership in civic affairs, educators may indeed assist in improving the power structure. This will pay rich dividends by assuring that school elections represent the will of basic citizen groups rather than the will of a few. However, this is an evolutionary matter. Educators will need to work for immediate school improvement using their understanding of the power structure. The development of quality schools is the educator's first priority as he assists in the long-range process of creating good government.

Suggested Readings

Agger, Robert E., Daniel Goldrich, and Bert Swanson. *The Rulers and the Ruled*. New York: John Wiley and Sons, 1964.

Bailey, Stephen K., Richard L. Frost, Paul E. Marsh, and Robert C. Wood. *Schoolmen and Politics*. Syracuse, N.Y.: Syracuse University Press, 1962.

Banfield, Edward C. *Political Influence*. New York: The Free Press, 1961.

Bell, Wendell, Richard Hill, and Charles R. Wright. *Public Leadership*. San Francisco: Chandler Publishing Company, 1961.

Dahl, Robert. *Who Governs?* New Haven: Yale University Press, 1961.

Form, William H., and Delbert C. Miller. *Industry, Labor, and Community*. New York: Harper and Row, 1960.

Hunter, Floyd. *Community Power Structure*. Chapel Hill: University of North Carolina Press, 1953.

Iannaccone, Lawrence, and Frank W. Lutz. *Politics, Power and Policy*. Columbus, Ohio: Charles E. Merrill Publishing Company, 1970.

Kimbrough, Ralph B. *Political Power and Educational Decision-Making*. Skokie, Ill.: Rand McNally and Company, 1964.

Kirst, Michael. *Politics of Education at the Local, State, and Federal Levels*. Berkeley, Cal.: McCutchan Publishing Corporation, 1970.

Masters, Nicholas A., et al. *State Politics and the Public Schools*. New York: Alfred A. Knopf, 1964.

Mills, C. Wright. *The Power Elite*. New York: Oxford University Press, 1956.

Presthus, Robert. *Men at the Top: A Study in Community Power*. New York: Oxford University Press, 1964.

Wirt, Frederick M. *Search for Community Power*. Englewood Cliffs, N.J.: Prentice-Hall, 1968.

Footnotes

1. Roe L. Johns and Ralph B. Kimbrough, *The Relationship of Socioeconomic Factors, Educational Leadership Patterns and Elements of Community Power Structure to Local Fiscal Policy* (Washington: U.S. Department of Health, Education, and Welfare, Office of Education, Bureau of Research, Cooperative Research Project No. 2842, 1968).

2. For a thorough analysis of political party functions, see Bernard R. Berelson, Paul F. Lazarsfeld, and William N. McPhee, *Voting* (Chicago: University of Chicago Press, 1954), Chapter 8.

3. Floyd Hunter, *Community Power Structure* (Chapel Hill: University of North Carolina Press, 1953).

4. David W. Minar, *Educational Decision-Making in Suburban Communities* (Evanston, Ill.: Northwestern University, Cooperative Research Project No. 2440, 1966).

5. Floyd Hunter, *op. cit.*

6. Robert A. Dahl, *Who Governs?* (New Haven: Yale University Press, 1961).

7. Robert Presthus, *Men at the Top: A Study in Community Power* (New York: Oxford University Press, 1964).

3

Understanding
Voting Behavior

The behavior of voters has a significant impact on the quality of education. Voters express their opinions through the election of school board members and through special elections concerning school policies. When educational leaders understand voter behavior in their school districts, they are in a better position to build strategies, to exert leadership, to influence elections, and to provide the conditions for quality education.

Students of government have made some classic studies of voter behavior that should be helpful to educators. There is also much written opinion on the subject. The best known and most widely quoted studies are about national campaigns for the presidency. Authorities have not conducted many in-depth studies of voter behavior in local and state school elections.Thus, care must be exercised in applying findings from studies of presidential elections to "non-partisan" school elections.

Previous election campaigns in the school district are excellent sources of information about voter behavior. Of special significance are the past school election campaigns in the district. These should be studied intensively. What were the campaign issues? Were there specific patterns of votes by geographic area, socioeconomic class, ethnic group, or other category? Was the popularity or unpopularity of the school board and superintendent an issue? What percentage of the eligible voters actually voted? What influence did organized group activity have upon public opinion? Who were the opinion leaders in the campaign? What were the major sources of political power in the campaigns? These are but a few of the questions that school leaders should answer in attempting to understand voter behavior in the school district.

School leaders should observe partisan conflicts in the district during school elections and during other referenda, such as elections for hospitals, streets, and roads. The more intensively the educator concentrates on voter behavior in several elections, especially the more recent ones, the more able he will be to plan effective campaign strategies for school elections.

Concepts of voter behavior developed by social scientists can be of considerable value to the education leader in organizing effective campaigns in school elections. Therefore, he needs to be conversant with terms such as "cross-pressures" that have grown out of these studies. The following section is designed to acquaint the reader with the concepts of the field of voting behavior. Fuller development of conceptual knowledge will be found in the suggested reading material at the end of this chapter.

Studies of Voting Behavior

Early studies of voting behavior were based on official election statistics. The poll results in voting precincts provide patterns that can be studied in the light of personalities and issues in election campaigns. For instance, one can generalize about the voting behavior of socioeconomic classes, rural or urban areas, ethnic groups, and other social groups by analyzing the voting statistics in precincts that encompass the different classifications of citizens. The official voting results also provide valuable insights into voter turnout and party preference. For instance, by studying past school elections, school executives can determine patterns of voting and nonvoting in different areas that give valuable clues to organized activity in future elections. Educators should study the school district participation patterns and be especially concerned with areas of high nonvoting patterns.

In a 1928 publication, Rice demonstrated the insights that may be obtained by studying official voting statistics.[1] He illustrated how progressive voting attitudes clustered within certain areas of a state. By concentrating on differences in attitudes, as measured by votes for or against progressive candidates, Rice was able to demonstrate a relationship between voting behavior and lines of communication. He concluded that political attitudes appeared to diffuse along transportation routes, railroads, and the like. Adjacent governmental units

tended to vote more alike if they were closely tied together by lines of communication.

Throughout this book we suggest that voter attitudes are as much a result of political activity as they are a basis of it. Rice probably observed results of the impact of leadership in the social system of the areas scrutinized. Interaction is a basic element in the development and continuance of social systems. Thus the educator may well detect important attitudes of leaders in political subsystems by studying voting statistics. A heavy vote against a school bond program in a precinct signals leadership activity within an attitudinal subsystem of the district. The educator must use such information in understanding politics and in building strategies for school improvement.

Studies of voting behavior have been strengthened by survey techniques. In the survey technique the problem of generalizing for the total population is simplified by studying a very small sample of voters. Inferences can be drawn about the total voting population of the nation by studying intensively the behavior of a scientifically selected sample of approximately 2,000 persons. In some studies, a scientifically drawn panel of voters is interviewed several times during an election campaign.

The Erie County Study

In 1944, Lazarsfeld, Berelson, and Gaudet published a memorable study of voting behavior entitled *The People's Choice*.[2] They applied survey techniques to the 1940 presidential election contest between Franklin Roosevelt and Wendell Willkie. Erie County, Ohio, was the setting for the study. Through sampling techniques, a panel of 600 persons was selected. They were interviewed about seven times during the 1940 election campaign. By repeated interviews, the investigators tried to identify psychological and social factors that influenced the voters. The main goal of the study was to determine how the mass media acted upon the attitudes of voters in the campaign. Explicit in the design was the idea that a voter decides among candidates as a buyer decides among products advertised through mass media. Findings in the study took the authors far afield of the merchandising concept.

Among the personality variables studied, none appeared to be significantly related to candidate choice. There was, however, a strong

relationship between candidate preference and socioeconomic status, religion, and rural or urban place of residence.

Only a few (54) of the voters on the panel of 600 persons changed candidate preferences during the campaign. Most of the voters had longstanding party attachments and decided early in the campaign how they would cast their ballots. Lazarsfeld and associates viewed attitude stability in voting as strengthening feelings of individual security. Furthermore, the development of common group political attitudes provided group reinforcement for persons in maintaining stable voting intentions.

Under what conditions do people change their vote during a political campaign? The Erie County research staff postulated that all persons carry around what were referred to as "half-forgotten" experiences that are in conflict with current voting intentions. Under certain conditions these experiences may be strengthened to produce a predisposition to change voting attitudes.

A much discussed discovery was what Lazarsfeld and associates called "cross-pressures." Persons who found themselves in inner conflict were likely to change their vote or withdraw from voting. Within the total context of his experience, a person is subject to cross-pressures that may cause him to feel that he should vote on both sides of an issue. Persons who experience change in social or economic status, for example, are likely to experience "in-betweenness" or cross-pressures. A poor boy who rises to upper middle class status is likely to feel pressures from conflicting political opinions.

The more a person feels cross-pressured, the more likely he is to manifest predispositions to change his vote, to decide not to vote in the campaign, or to decide late in the campaign how he will vote.

Voters often find themselves in the midst of inconsistency. For example, they may be attracted to a particular candidate but basically disagree with his stand on an issue in domestic affairs. These inconsistencies may be solved by either (1) playing down the significance of the issue, or (2) perceiving that the candidate does not really disagree in substance with the voter's attitudes.

The major contribution of the Erie County research was to portray voting behavior as a social phenomenon. Earlier writers on voting behavior had emphasized the dynamics of the individual to the exclusion of his relationship to the dynamics of groups. Lazarsfeld and associates presented a model of voting behavior as an aspect of a complex social system.

The last chapter of *The People's Choice*, entitled "The Nature of Personal Influence," has been widely quoted. In it, the authors highlighted concepts of voter behavior in the social context. Within the complex social system were opinion leaders — those who tended to legitimize political opinion among their following. There was a two-step flow of political communication — from the mass media to the opinion leaders to the less active citizens. The opinion leaders were in effect interpreters to their following of what was transmitted via radio, newspapers, and other sources of printed information. Thus, the opinion leaders (elsewhere referred to as influentials or power-wielders) had great impact on voter behavior in the campaign.

The personal nature of influence on voter behavior was stressed in the elaboration of the findings. A large majority of those voting who had not expected to vote stated that personal influence changed their original plans. Those who changed their vote frequently cited the personal influence of friends, relatives, and others as responsible. The person-to-person nature of influence in the election made a lasting impression on the research group. As a consequence, much of the elaboration of the findings consisted of extolling the advantages of person-to-person influence over the influence of the mass media.

The reader may question whether concepts developed from a presidential election have anything in common with school elections. The answer is that these concepts are directly applicable to school elections. For example, the stability of voter opinion found in the Erie County study was also found by Agger in a school election study in Eugene, Oregon. (Agger's study is discussed later in this section. See page 49.)

The concept that voter opinion probably will not change radically during the election campaign is important to educators. Voters tend to decide early in the campaign how they are going to vote. This emphasizes the need for intensive preelection activity by schoolmen to establish favorable public opinion, and the need for accurate public opinion polls prior to and early in the campaign. On the other hand, the stability of voter opinion suggests that there is a need for greater emphasis on organization in political campaigns, in order for educators to influence more voters to change their vote for improvement projects.

Here again, the Erie County study provides some important concepts. Persons who are cross-pressured are likely to change opinions during the campaign; they are also less likely to vote on election day

than other voters. The educator who has intimate knowledge of which persons are most subject to cross-pressures can plan his campaign strategy to encourage vote changes during the campaign.

Perhaps the greatest contribution of the Erie County study was the concept of personal influence — the idea that opinion leaders had great personal influence on voter opinion. If educators desire functional power in election campaigns, they must work closely with those who can make school proposals acceptable in the district, as was discussed in Chapter 2. Well-run campaigns for school proposals must include the exercise of personal influence at the grassroots level. Personal influence exercised through the informal, face-to-face groups in the community is most effective and will have more impact than the exclusive use of mass media.

The Elmira Study

In the 1948 presidential election (Truman versus Dewey), Berelson, Lazarsfeld and McPhee did a followup study, applying the panel method in Elmira, New York.[3] They attempted to anticipate the psychological and social influences on voter behavior as a basis for repeated interviews with the panel during the election campaign. In their report of this study they recognized that certain social conditions influenced voting: "The individual's vote is the product of a number of social conditions or influences: his socioeconomic and ethnic affiliations, his family tradition, his personal associations, his attitudes on the issues of the day, his membership in formal organizations."[4]

Community leaders exhibit much interest in the role of organizations in political activity. The Elmira group studied organizational activity intensively and found that the preponderance of organizations did not participate in the 1948 campaign.[5] The organizations, by and large, did not actively try to change voter behavior. People tended to belong to organizations in which the membership was congruent with their own political opinions. Organizational membership probably did create political interest among persons who otherwise would have been less interested in the presidential campaign. The organizations functioned to bring people together and increase interaction among leaders in the community. This could serve as a medium either to reinforce opinion or to change opinion. The political parties were largely concerned with routine administrative details

in the campaign. Party workers were not ideological leaders in Elmira.

Voter behavior did relate to socioeconomic class, religious group,
and ethnic group in the Elmira study. These findings are reviewed
only briefly here because their direct application to school elections
is of questionable value. Persons in upper socioeconomic classes tended to vote Republican. Native-born Protestants voted Republican
more often than Italian Americans, Jews, and Negroes. Catholics
tended to vote Democratic regardless of national origin. Catholics
who participated often in civic activities tended to vote Democratic
less often than Catholics who were apathetic in civic affairs. There
were noticeable differences between older and younger voters. For
instance, young Catholics were more Republican than their elders,
and young Protestants tended to vote Democratic more often than
their elders.

Berelson and associates reiterated the often repeated finding that
family tradition is reflected in voting behavior — there was a high
degree of agreement on voting preference in family systems. Considerable homogeneity was also evident between voting preference and
choices of friends. Thus, as indicated in numerous studies, informal
associations of persons (e.g., cliques, work groups, friends) have a
powerful influence on voting behavior. Many of these groups in a
community are characterized by homogeneity of political opinion.

Persons who talked with others who agreed with their opinion
were likely to remain firm in their original conviction. Those who did
not recall any political discussions usually did not vote. Persons reporting discussions with the opposition tended to defect to the opposition in voting behavior. Thus, participation in political activity and
patterns of interaction molded voter opinion. These concepts have
fundamental meaning for organizing election campaigns for schools.

The Elmira study also reemphasized the concept of cross-pressures,
as discussed in the Erie County study.

The 1952 Michigan Survey Research Center Study

The University of Michigan Survey Research Center undertook a
study of the 1952 presidential election based on a national sample of
approximately 2,000 persons.[6] Those in the sample were interviewed
twice — just before and immediately after the election. The researchers did not emphasize sociological variables influencing voter be-

havior as had the investigators in the Erie County and Elmira studies, but rather the psychological attitudes of the individual that caused him to vote for the candidate of his choice. Voters were believed to be influenced greatly by three variables: (1) party identification, (2) issue orientation, and (3) attraction to the candidate.

The extent to which the individual identified himself as a Republican or Democrat was a strong psychological force in voting behavior. Thus, the person who considered himself a strong Democrat or strong Republican was likely to vote for the candidate of his party, while those who were "nominal" party members did not vote as consistently within one party.

The voters' attitudes toward issues were related to their presidential preference. The extent of issue orientation was also significantly related to participation in the election.

The extent of the voter's personal attraction to the candidates was also related to both his participation and his preference. The research staff reported the following conclusion:

We have found that those people who felt themselves strongly identified with one of the major parties, held strongly partisan views on issues which were consistent with those of their party, and were strongly attracted by the personal attributes of their party's candidate expressed preference in nearly every case for the candidate their party put forward.[7]

These concepts of individual behavior in elections can be useful to educators, as the following example illustrates:

A school election was held several years ago in a Florida school district to increase expenditures for education. In this particular district the school superintendent and certain school board members had become very unpopular. As the campaign proceeded, the real issue became not the proposed expenditures for education, but rather whether a new superintendent should be appointed and changes made in membership on the board of education.

The citizens of the school district were repelled by their perceptions of the personal attributes of those who were publicly campaigning for school improvement. Large numbers of them voted against the proposal because they were not personally attracted to the school superintendent, and the proposal failed. This lack of personal attraction was one of the most important factors contributing to the negative vote.

The Theory of Alienation and Voter
Behavior in School Elections

When people vote negatively on certain school proposals, educators often express the opinion that they are "hitting back" at something or someone. For instance, a voter might be thought to vote against a school millage increase as a way of expressing his displeasure with taxing decisions at the national level. Another expression of this view is that the negative voters of a school district were acting from feelings of helplessness and dissatisfaction with things as they exist. These statements express the theory of alienation or of mass society, which has been very popular among some social scientists and in the popular press.

According to the theory of alienation, many citizens often have feelings of disenfranchisement or powerlessness in industrialized society. They do not comprehend existing socioeconomic conditions, and from their perspective the world has become irrational. This view is coupled with feelings of frustration. These people become increasingly isolated from the mainstream.[8] Having no firm basis for personal action and lacking in self-confidence, these citizens are highly susceptible to movements based on oversimplified statements of position and high emotional appeal.

Crain, Katz, and Rosenthal have challenged those who place great emphasis on the theory of alienation in explaining voter behavior in local governmental elections.[9] They question the conclusions, reached by Horton and Thompson, that alienation was the primary factor explaining negative votes against school bond issues in two communities in New York.[10]

Crain and associates concentrated their research on water fluoridation referenda, obtaining information via questionnaire from approximately 700 cities. They reached the conclusion that the theory of alienation, while it was one factor, was invalid as the primary explanation of voter behavior in water fluoridation elections. These researchers present persuasive logical arguments for their position as well as data to support their contention. In the process they expound concepts that should be very useful to educators. While educational elections may have different characteristics from water fluoridation referenda, there is enough similarity for useful correlation.

Crain and associates suggest that most political observers, including educators, tend to assume that what is proposed in public referenda is logical beyond question. Consequently, anyone who opposes the

logically conceived school millage election is assumed to be wrong. The chief motive in most analyses is to find how the person voting negatively was misled or became such an odd fellow in the first place. With these basic assumptions, it is easy to interpret the postelection statements of citizens as expressing the tenets of the alienation theory. If we assume that the proposal is the only valid one possible, then persons who do not support it are naturally somehow estranged.

Crain and associates also explored why there has been so much difference in the vote results among different cities. Why, they asked, has fluoridation passed by big majorities in some cities and failed miserably in others? They suggest that if voters are alienated in the industrialized society, as the theory is expressed, they should be more equally alienated among the cities in which referenda were held. If alienation is the primary factor, most differences in election results from one school district to another should not occur.

Crain and associates found that several factors were related to election outcomes in water fluoridation proposals: the political structure of communities, the actions of civic and elected community leaders, socioeconomic characteristics of the communities, and levels of controversy generated in the campaigns.

Of considerable significance was the finding that the failure of elected and civic leaders to support fluoridation actively often resulted in defeat of the proposals in referenda. Low levels of controversy, active support of health organizations, and forceful leadership from community influentials characterized elections in which the vote was favorable to fluoridation.

The fluoridation study has some important implications for educators. They should not assume that they have the only logically defensible position, and that everyone who opposes it is some kind of extremist. Such an attitude may cause educators to be unnecessarily defensive and overconfident. Active endorsement of educational proposals by civic and elected community influentials is essential. Forthright support by the influentials will help legitimize the school board proposal and possibly curtail opposition that could lead to high-level controversy. Support of proposals by community organizations is also helpful.

Moreover, the validity of a proposal is not the only factor in its acceptance or rejection. In a great many instances professional men assume that a proposal that is logical to them will be immediately logical to any citizen. As a consequence, they have a tendency to

overlook the significance of the political process in presenting the proposal to the public. Most educational proposals of the future will not be accepted without question or substantiation. They will have to be legitimized.

Voter Participation in School Elections

A study of voter behavior in a school referendum was made in Eugene, Oregon, by Agger.[11] The election issue was initiation of a kindergarten program financed by public funds. Two polls were taken: a preelection poll nine months before the election, and a postelection poll five weeks after the election.

Agger's conclusions are very similar to those reached in the studies of nonschool election voter behavior. He found surprising stability in opinion among voters throughout the campaign: 73 percent of the voters who expressed favorable opinions nine months before the elections voted for the kindergarten program; 75 percent of those who express unfavorable opinions in the poll voted against kindergartens.

Of considerable interest to educators is Agger's analysis of voter groups for and against kindergartens. The less educated persons who voted opposed kindergartens by a 10 to 1 majority; moderately educated persons who voted opposed kindergartens by a 65 percent to 35 percent margin: but highly educated persons voting favored the program by a 52 percent to 48 percent margin. Analysis of opinions among the nonvoters favored the kindergarten program in all categories. Therefore, Agger reached the conclusion that the school proposal failed not because more of the citizens opposed kindergartens but because more of those who voted opposed the program. A different vote would have been realized by getting out the vote among those favoring kindergartens.

In a study conducted by a group at Stanford University, 900 registered voters were interviewed before and after a school bond election.[12] The research group also conducted several thousand interviews with voters in numerous school districts to determine their attitudes toward schools, how they participated in school affairs, and how the schools communicated with them.

The attitudes of voters toward school costs and their evaluation of the local schools were closely associated with the likelihood of voting. Other attitudes that could be important in voter preference in bond elections concerned the economic consequences of the elec-

tion, pride in the schools, evaluation of teachers, and teaching of the "3 R's."

The voter expressing the most favorable attitude toward schools was the young, skilled, clerical or sales worker with a child of school age who had resided in the community a short time. The voter who had the most unfavorable attitude was the young, highly educated, professional or technician who was a long-time resident of the community. This is probably a manifestation of effects of the group interaction, family, and friendship ties highlighted in the Elmira study.

About half of the voters showed no evidence of participating in school affairs and indicated no interest in the schools. Only one-third of the voters took an active part in school affairs. About 11 percent indicated an interest in schools but did not participate. Some 6 percent took part in school matters but were not especially interested in schools. The voters who participated in school affairs were more knowledgeable about the educational system.

Analyses of school-community communication patterns provided some significant insights. For example, the voters who voted favorably on school bond issues were likely to view school officials as sources of information.

Applying Voter Behavior Concepts

What implications do the findings of research about voter behavior have for the organization of school election campaigns. In answering this question, ten generalizations from the research are presented and discussed.

The authors reiterate that voter behavior is different in different school districts. The factor contributing most heavily to voter behavior in school district A may not be significant in district B. Therefore, schoolmen should make a careful study of the applicability of each of the voter behavior concepts for the political dynamics of their particular school districts.

1. The act of voting is more likely a sociological phenomenon than an individual decision.

The idea of each voter in a secret voting booth, acting by his own individual conscience, is largely a popular myth. In the Erie County and Elmira studies, the research teams found much evidence that

members of informal groups (cliques, ethnic associations, crowds, etc.) tended to vote alike. In other words, voters tend to vote like those with whom they interact often. In Chapter 2 we emphasized that all complex political systems are made up of many informal and formal subsystems. These subsystems have boundaries. They have hierarchies of opinion leaders, status leaders, and followers. The voters' opinions and attitudes in elections are influenced through their participation in these systems.

Voting may be a group activity, for the most part. If educators are going to influence voter attitudes, they must organize to influence various specific social systems in the district. This requires a carefully planned organization. School leaders must identify the systems, analyze their interaction patterns, know their opinion leaders, and find ways to intervene in the system's thought processes.

2. Personal influence is a very powerful and persuasive force acting on voters during election campaigns.

In planning election campaigns, educators must not overlook the person-to-person nature of political influence. This influence is exercised through the interaction patterns and opinion leadership hierarchies of the school district's complex social system. It is in the numerous interacting subsystems of the structure that personal influence is exercised. Schoolmen will not win elections consistently by simply mobilizing the mass media every time the approval of the electorate is required. Effective political activity involves the exercise of personal leadership within the political system and its subsystems. The undecided voter responds positively to personal leadership. The messages of mass media undergo interpretation by opinion leaders in the system. Consequently, a well-run political campaign must be organized right down to the grassroots.

3. The personal influence of influentials (opinion leaders) may be a critical factor in legitimizing (making acceptable) school proposals among voters.

Chapter 2 emphasized the significance of influentials in community decision-making. These people are highly respected by many voters. They are articulate. They are centers of communication nets in the political system. They have established their positions in some instances through many years of leadership. They are key communicators of political attitudes and opinions among a following. Schoolmen may be able to win campaigns without the public support of these leaders, but their active support can assure a much greater

acceptability for school proposals. Their active opposition might well mean defeat of important proposals.

4. The most critical subsystems molding voter attitudes may be informal.

Too often we make the formal groups our targets and ignore the vast opinion-molding power of informal groups. The Elmira study found that the preponderance of organizations did little in the presidential campaign.[13] This finding is consistent with other studies. For example, in Presthus's study of two cities in New York, only 5 of 80 organizations contacted were active in the school bond issues.[14] Consequently, in organizing for school elections, school leaders need to influence the opinion leaders and followers of informal cliques, crowds, friendship associations, and power groups. These may likely be the sources of power that control the activity of formal organizations.

5. Many voters make up their minds about school election issues very early in the campaign.

This is a very important concept and emphasizes the need for polling. The studies of election campaigns show that the opinions of many voters are stable. Citizens tend not to change their preferences during an election campaign, probably because of conformity patterns and reinforcement by the social systems that the voter inhabits during the campaign. This suggests that school campaigns to mold opinion must begin very early — probably before the campaign is officially announced by the board of education. To do this, favorable public-school relations must be developed before the campaign.

The absence of opinion change of voters in the Erie County and Elmira studies may well indicate that presidential candidates of the 1940 and 1952 campaigns had not learned how to intervene and influence the "group mind" of informal social systems. They depended greatly on mass media and political party workers. The authors believe that a highly developed, personalized leadership approach can change voter opinion about school issues. Most persons can be influenced by those in whom they trust and have confidence. We believe that strategies can be developed to influence the opinion leaders of the political power system and its interacting subsystems, by person-to-person leadership. Political games are won by the tireless work of the down-the-line political leaders, not by a few flashy "backfield" persons holding microphones in their hands. The details of organizing political campaigns are discussed in Chapter 5.

6. Persons who feel cross-pressured are likely to react by (a) vacillating on the issue, (b) withdrawing from voting, or (c) deciding late in the campaign how to vote.

This concept has far-ranging implications. In some communities school leaders should deliberately plan their strategy to raise an issue that will produce cross-pressures in many people. For example, some school districts are characterized by a high degree of consensus, and citizens tend to vote consistently to keep the status quo. The vote can be changed in many such districts only by deliberately creating opposing forces that result in cross-pressures within many voters.

In other communities, however, the best strategy may be to play down conflict between opposing forces. For example, in a school district with a traditionally favorable vote for school improvement, the creation of severe conflict could cause significant changes in voter preference and withdrawal of voter support for schools.

7. Socioeconomic status may influence voter preference in school election campaigns.

Contrary to popular belief, not all people have favorable opinions about the great value of education. Studies have shown that many "downtrodden" socioeconomic groups have a "sour grapes" attitude toward schooling. Young voters in the upper and upper-middle social classes are more likely to participate voluntarily in school elections than persons in lower and lower-lower social classes. Persons who move from one social class to another class are likely to reflect changes in voting patterns and conceivably could change their attitudes toward the value of education.

8. Family ties are significant in voting.

Studies show a high degree of agreement within families. The family is, of course, a close-knit social system within which communication is frequent and meaningful. Contrary to popular opinion, the influence of families is not restricted to rural areas. Kinship ties have been shown to be significant influences in large urban centers.[15] Consequently, schoolmen should be sensitive to the kinship systems of the district. Knowledge of opinion leaders in these systems and functional contact with them about school needs could make a significant difference in the ballot box results.

9. Persons who are actively involved in civic affairs often vote independently and in opposition to informal group opinion.

Numerous writers stress the importance of encouraging widespread citizen involvement in educational programs. This is obviously a

means of assisting people to vote independently, regardless of family ties, friendship patterns, cliques, and other informal sources of influence. Voters who take part directly in school affairs tend to feel that schools are trying to do a good job.[16] They are more likely to take cues in school elections from school officials or other active, informed participants supportive of quality schools.

10. Although alienation is one factor that produces negative votes, it may have been too greatly emphasized by schoolmen to the neglect of other significant factors.

The Crain, Katz, and Rosenthal study of water fluoridation indicated that the theory of alienation was not as important in producing negative votes as many writers have claimed.[17] This is not to say that alienation is not a factor. It is an important consideration. At the same time, educators should not use it to explain away their inability to obtain acceptance of educational ideas among voters. It is too easy for a school official to blame the defeat of a school proposal on the large number of estranged, negative voters than to admit that his proposal was faulty or that his planning and campaign strategy were disorganized.

The study by Crain and associates identified factors other than alienation that may also be of significance in voting behavior. For instance, the outcomes of fluoridation elections were heavily dependent on the active support and leadership of community influentials. Another factor, emphasized in Chapter 2, was the shape of politics in the community. The activity of organizations, socioeconomic characteristics of the cities studied, and levels of controversy associated with the election were other important factors.

The authors are not contending that the theory of alienation is not useful, but that too much weight may be placed upon alienation among the many factors contributing to election results. Certainly many voters do become estranged and may well take a negative attitude toward school board proposals. However, is it simply alienation or is it an indication that the people have lost confidence in the board, the professional administrators, or both? The existence of a credibility gap hardly meets the criteria for a classic case of alienation.

Dealing with Psychological Variables

The Michigan Survey Research Center study identified three

psychological variables associated with voter behavior: (1) the person's identification with a political party; (2) the voter's conception of the issues; and (3) the voter's personal attraction to the candidate. These variables from the world of partisan politics may appear to be foreign to the world of nonpartisan school politics. Yet we may well explore their possible application to school elections.

In the typical school district, educators have a following. This following could be conceptualized as a school "party." In a school district characterized by severe conflict, an antiestablishment crowd appears that is opposed to the educational policies of the "school crowd." Let us treat the "proschool crowd" and "antischool crowd" followings as being political parties. They may not be organized parties; however, they do have leadership hierarchies and "party lines." Applying the voter behavior concept, the degree of the citizen's attachment to either partisan group (i.e., strong, nominal, or weak feelings of attachment) will influence his voting behavior in school elections. Persons having strong "party" attachments are more likely to vote in school elections than those with nominal feelings. Those who do vote and have strong identification with the school following will vote in favor of school progress.

The results of the Stanford study support this concept.[18] The citizens who voted for bond issues were more likely to have talked with school officials and viewed these officials as important sources of information. This is indicative of a school following in the districts surveyed.

Regardless of opposition or lack of opposition in most school districts, there is a school following — the parents and other citizens who are keenly interested in good schools and participate actively in school affairs. This following acts like a political party when school elections are conducted. The success or lack of success of school elections may depend upon the extent of attachment of community leaders and citizens to the school following. Thus, elections are often won or lost by educators long before an election contest is joined. Experienced schoolmen may refer to the strength of their following by such terms as "good public relations" or "poor public relations." What they really mean is the extent to which people identify with the objectives of school officials.

The voter's conception of the issues in school elections constitutes the second psychological variable. Orientation to the issues is related to participation. The voter's attitudes concerning issues of school

costs and the needs of schools will influence his behavior. He sees school policies in the context of the economic and social systems. Voters may be cross-pressured by being strongly attracted to those favoring school improvement but in personal disagreement with increased school costs. Voters whose feelings toward the schools are consistent with the educational issues presented usually vote with the "proschool party."

The third psychological variable in the Michigan study was the voter's attraction to the candidate. In many school elections the school superintendent (or the school board) plays the role of a candidate in a partisan election. In other words, many people vote on the basis of their feelings toward the school superintendent, teachers, or members of the board of education, and the welfare of schools is of secondary significance. School elections are often won or lost because of the popularity of the superintendent or board of education. The authors have personally observed that the attraction of citizens to the chief school officer or the board of education is a significant factor in school elections. This has important implications in deciding who should be the main spokesman for school propositions. The public leader for any school proposal may well be perceived as a candidate for office is perceived.

The implications of the Michigan study for school elections may be paraphrased as follows: Voters who are strongly identified with a school following, hold views on the election issues that are consistent with the views of this following, and are strongly attracted to the personal attributes of the main spokesman for the school improvement project, will participate and vote favorably for the schools.

Perception plays a big role in helping the voter reduce personal inconsistency among the three psychological variables. For instance, suppose a very conservative voter has a strong attachment to the members of a board of education. A multimillion-dollar proposal by the board would throw him into some conflict. He values his friendship with the board, but opposes increased costs. Let us assume that he also has strong association with other leaders who are actively supporting the board proposal. The voter may resolve his personal inconsistency by (1) playing down the significance of the proposal's cost, (2) perceiving that the proposal is really consistent with his own beliefs, or (3) perceiving that the spokesmen for the bond issue are really in agreement with his own position.

The Stanford study illustrated that voters have different attitudes

toward schools, that many people do not take part in educational affairs, and that voter behavior in school elections is not dependent solely on attitudes toward education.[19] For example, the voter's attitudes toward costs and economic consequences was associated with his likelihood of voting in school referenda. Occupational, age, family status, and residence differences gave rise to different voter behavior patterns.

The Stanford findings seem to reflect general civic (group) influences on voter attitudes. They do not mean that persons of one occupation will have favorable attitudes and those of another occupation unfavorable attitudes. Several factors combine to create attitudes.

Length of residence was probably a decisive factor, because short-time residents are not as readily influenced by longstanding community norms and group dynamics. Nevertheless, these observations demonstrate that the attitude of voters about schools can be identified and that these attitudes influence voter behavior in school elections.

Education leaders should be sensitive to the opinions of voters. Polls should be used to assess these opinions formally. Strategies should be developed to influence voter opinions in favor of schools. No political campaign should be employed without knowledge of voter opinion.

The Stanford study also demonstrated the widespread lack of genuine interest of voters in school affairs. Furthermore, there was a shockingly low level of active involvement in educational affairs. Educators must do something about this situation. If half of the people who bother to register do not vote in school elections, schoolmen are failing to provide fitting campaign strategies. Democratic decision-making depends on viable citizen participation.

Suggested Readings

Berelson, Bernard R., Paul Lazarsfeld, and William N. McPhee. *Voting*. Chicago: University of Chicago Press, 1954.

Burdick, Eugene, and Arthur J. Brodbeck (eds.). *American Voting Behavior*. Glencoe, Ill.: The Free Press, 1959.

Campbell, Angus, Gerald Gurin, and Warren E. Miller. *The Voter Decides*. Evanston, Ill.: Row, Peterson and Company, 1954.

Carter, Richard F. *Voters and Their Schools*. Stanford: Institute for

Communication Research, Stanford University, U.S. Office of Education Cooperative Research Project No. 308, 1960.

Crain, Robert L., Elihu Katz, and Donald B. Rosenthal. *The Politics of Community Conflict: The Fluoridation Decision.* New York: Bobbs-Merrill Company, 1969.

Lazarsfeld, Paul F., Bernard R. Berelson, and Hazel Gaudet. *The People's Choice.* New York: Columbia University Press, 1948.

Footnotes

1. Stuart A. Rice, *Quantitative Methods in Politics* (New York: Alfred A. Knopf, 1928).

2. Paul F. Lazarsfeld, Bernard R. Berelson, and Hazel Gaudet, *The People's Choice* (New York: Columbia University Press, 1948).

3. Bernard R. Berelson, Paul F. Lazarsfeld, and William N. McPhee, *Voting* (Chicago: University of Chicago Press, 1954), p. 37.

4. *Ibid.*

5. *Ibid.*, pp. 51—52.

6. Angus Campbell, Gerald Gurin, and Warren E. Miller, *The Voter Decides* (Evanston, Ill.: Row, Peterson and Company, 1954).

7. *Ibid.*, pp. 182—83.

8. Melvin Seeman, "On the Meaning of Alienation," *American Sociological Review*, vol. 24, no. 6 (December 1959), pp. 783—90.

9. Robert L. Crain, Elihu Katz, and Donald B. Rosenthal, *The Politics of Community Conflict: The Fluoridation Decision* (New York: Bobbs-Merrill Company, 1969).

10. John E. Horton and Wayne E. Thompson, "Powerlessness and Political Negativism," *American Journal of Sociology*, vol. 67, no. 5 (March 1962), pp. 485—93.

11. Robert E. Agger, "The Politics of Local Education," in Alan Rosenthal (ed.), *Governing Education: A Reader on Politics, Power, and Public School Policy* (Garden City, N.Y.: Doubleday and Company, 1969).

12. Richard F. Carter, *Voters and Their Schools* (Stanford: Institute for Communication Research, Stanford University, U.S. Office of Education Cooperative Research Project No. 308, 1960).

13. Berelson, et al., *op. cit.*, pp. 51—52.

14. Robert Presthus, *Men at the Top: A Study in Community Power* (New York: Oxford University Press, 1964), p. 266.

15. Scott Greer, "Individual Participation in Mass Society," in Roland Young (ed.), *Approaches to the Study of Politics* (Evanston, Ill.: Northwestern University Press, 1958).

16. Carter, *op. cit.*, p. 12.

17. Crain, et al., *op. cit.*

18. Carter, *op. cit.*

19. *Ibid.*

4

Public Opinion Polling

In the world of politics the use of feedback is essential. Feedback is input from the environment to the organization. For example, when the leadership of the school system announces plans to include sex education in the curriculum (output) there will be citizen communication to the organization as a reaction (input).

Feedback is the way by which persons in the organization learn how well the organization is doing in the environment. It furnishes a steering mechanism. Citizen communication to an organization may be unsolicited, solicited on a "catch as catch can" basis, or solicited in a systematic fashion. In many organizations the feedback process is faulty — persons in the organization ignore significant inputs, twist the meaning of negative inputs, fail to obtain and process feedback in an objective, organized fashion, or commit other errors.

In modern political campaigns opinion polls are used to secure feedback. Considerable effort is devoted to carefully planning and executing polls to insure that a properly selected group of voters is contacted, their opinions are solicited in a structured fashion, the opinions obtained are analyzed in an objective manner, and the data are carefully considered in choosing campaign tactics. School elections, like other kinds of elections, have several uses for polls.

Polls can be used as a basis for deciding whether a school election is advisable at a given time. Assume that the leaders of a school district are considering asking the electorate to approve an increase in the district's operating levy, to provide additional funds for establishing kindergartens in the district. A carefully determined sample of voters might be queried to determine their reaction to increasing taxes to provide kindergartens. If analysis of the results of the poll

indicated that most of the people in the sample (a) did not know the present status of kindergartens in the district, (b) were generally dissatisfied with how the existing funds were being used, (c) could not identify many benefits of kindergartens, and (d) were opposed to a tax increase for such purposes, the appropriate decision would probably be to delay the request for an increased levy until a more favorable climate for kindergartens has been developed.

Polls taken during the election campaign can tell strategists what effect their political activities are having on public opinion. Suppose that in the early days of a school election campaign school leaders divided their efforts fairly equally between television and newspaper ads and personal contact (coffees, small group meetings, etc.). A poll is taken and it is found that those people who have been reached by the personal contact are more knowledgeable about the issues and more favorably inclined toward the school leaders' point of view. Such a finding should indicate to the strategists that increased emphasis should be placed on personal contact. Thus, polling provides a basis for exercising flexibility in the choice of techniques that prove to be paying off and discontinuance of activities that are costing votes.

Polls may also be used to discover why a proposal sponsored by school leadership was rejected by the electorate. For example, if a district-sponsored proposal for a bond issue for new school buildings is narrowly defeated, an analysis of the election results may show that the defeat can be attributed in large measure to a 60 percent to 70 percent negative vote in 11 of the 65 voting precincts. A sample of voters from each of the 11 precincts could be selected and polled to determine who voted against the proposal and why. The data obtained could be used as a basis for a public information campaign designed to build a more favorable climate for future district-sponsored proposals.

In the past, many school leaders relied on inaccurate "horseback" procedures to make their political judgments. This is no longer adequate. Through modern polling techniques schoolmen can know very accurately what the voters think at a given time. Therefore, the authors devote this lengthy chapter to a discussion of opinion polling techniques and their use in modern political campaigns. We do not intend to suggest that feedback obtained by systematically conducted polls should be substituted for feedback obtained by contact with community influentials, municipal officials, labor group leaders,

teacher group leaders, mass media personnel, and the like. Feedback obtained by both means should be used in school elections.

Assessing the pulse of the public in relation to local school district matters is not a new activity of school leaders. The opinions of the public have in the past been sought to determine public needs, public expectations of the local school district, the degree of acceptance of the district and its programs, public understanding of the problems of the district, how the public receives information about the district, reactions to major visible issues, and reactions to proposals, bond issues, and millage levies. In recent years there have been several efforts to determine the tolerance of the community for innovation and experimentation within the local school district. Far too often, however, the opinion-seeking efforts of school leaders have been marked by lack of sophistication, which has resulted in serious errors in assessing the "public pulse." Lack of sophistication has manifested itself in the purposes of the polling, sampling methodology, development of data-gathering techniques (instrumentation), and failure to differentiate between attitude determination and opinion polling.

For purposes of the present discussion, an attitude may be defined as a hypothetical construct representing a person's predisposition to evaluate some aspect (a person, issue, object, or symbol) of his environment in a positive or negative manner. Opinion is an overt verbal expression by a person about a specific phenomenon at a given point in time and under a given set of circumstances. Opinions reflect attitudes. However, they are less stable and may be influenced by internal attitude conflicts. For example, a citizen may be favorably disposed toward education, the activities of the local school district, and the local school district chief executive as a person. He may at the same time have a predisposition to look unfavorably upon deficit spending, expanded social welfare programs by schools, and extended governmental interference into the affairs of individuals. If the citizen is asked whether he will vote for an increase in the local school district millage levy immediately following a positive event associated with the school district or its chief executive, he may respond in a favorable manner. However, the same citizen if asked the same question following an exposure to proposals for deficit financing by other governmental agencies may respond in a negative manner.

Furthermore, attitudes not expressed verbally may be expressed by

nonverbal behavior. Thus, a person may express an opinion in one direction and behave in a manner contrary to the verbal expression. This may be a function of his inability to articulate an attitude or his failure to recognize an attitude at the conscious level.

The foregoing suggests that the process of instrument development is more complex if the public polling is aimed at determining attitudes than if the polling seeks to solicit opinions. In opinion polling, a series of well-developed items may be adequate to determine opinions, whereas in determining attitudes it is necessary to insure that the series of items constitutes a scale. Designing an attitude scale requires the application of fairly complex statistical processes. The focus of the present discussion is opinion polling, not attitude measurement. There may be times when attitude determination is imperative for school leaders engaged in trying to win a school election. If so, the authors suggest that professional assistance be sought from a nearby university or a management consulting firm that specializes in attitude measurement.

In public opinion polling on issues that may be the subject of school elections, attention must be given to defining purposes, sampling, methods of contact, data-gathering instruments, organizing and conducting polls, and using data from polls. These are the subjects of the sections that follow. The authors have made effort to limit technical discourse and detail in the discussion. If further detail and technical explanation are desired, the reader is invited to refer to the suggested readings at the end of the chapter. Also, if within the local school district there are no persons possessing the needed expertise for conducting polls, employment of specialists on a consultant basis is recommended. The cost will be modest when viewed in light of the grievous errors in judgment that may result from a poorly conducted public opinion poll.

Defining the Purposes of the Poll

Far too often when a public opinion poll is taken in a local school district, only cursory attention is given to the purposes to be served by the poll, or the purposes are stated in terms far too loose and generalized to provide the needed direction. In either instance it is quite likely that the wrong or an unnecessary segment of the public will be polled, irrelevant questions will be asked, and data will be improperly analyzed. Such errors are costly in both time and money.

In defining the purposes of the poll, care should be taken to be explicit — about the people whose opinions are sought, about the issues for which the polling is conducted, and about such matters as comparisons within and among groups, if these are desired.

Let us assume that school leaders are interested in knowing whether they can expect at least 51 percent of the voters voting in the next school millage election to vote in favor of a five mill increase in the local operating levy for schools. They might define the purpose of the polling as:

Are the people of the school district willing to see more money spent in support of schools?

Such a statement of purpose is practically useless. It does not consider: What people? What schools? How much more money? When? For what purposes will the money be used? What method of revenue raising is being considered and from what level of government? The purpose as stated does not even suggest that additional taxes must be levied if more money is to be spent for schools. The purpose would be more adequately stated:

1. Ninety days before the next annual Zach Township School District operating millage election, what percent of the registered voters of Zach Township say they (a) definitely plan to vote in the next school millage election, (b) definitely plan not to vote in the next millage election, (c) will probably vote in the next millage election, (d) will probably not vote in the next millage election, (e) do not know whether they will vote in the next millage election?

2. Of those persons saying they will definitely or will probably vote in the next millage election, what pecentage say they (a) will definitely vote in favor of the five mill increase over the present operating levy for the Zach Township School District, (b) will definitely vote against such a levy, (c) think they will vote in favor of such a levy, (d) think they will vote against such a levy, (e) do not know whether they will vote in favor of or against such a levy?

In this statement of purpose, adequate direction is provided for defining the population to be polled, the questions to be asked, and the types of data analysis that will be necessary. Taking the illustration one step further, let us suppose that as a basis for planning campaign strategy school leaders are interested in determining the distributions of opinions among the voters planning to vote by age categories, occupational groups, and places of residence. If so, these purposes should be stated so that the needed age, occupational, and residence groups will be represented in the sample, the data will be

collected from the respondents, and tabulations of opinions will be done by the categories specified. In other words, if the poll is intended to determine the distributions of opinion of the several "publics" in a school district, which is often desirable, the statement of purposes of the poll should specifically indicate this intent. The school leaders could, in effect, determine the opinions of the "55 years of age and older public," the "blue collar public," the "public of the 7th precinct," the "55 years of age and older, blue collar, 7th precinct public," and so on.

In defining purposes for polling, it is essential to avoid words that are subject to numerous interpretations and to use words that are subject to few interpretations. For example, in planning for a millage election, school leaders may be interested in finding out what the voters who plan to vote in the next millage election know about the financing of the Zach Township School District. They might define their purposes as:

1. Do the voters planning to vote in the next school millage election in Zach Township really understand how the Zach Township School District schools are financed?

2. Do the voters planning to vote in the next school millage election in Zach Township appreciate the financial plight of the Zach Township schools?

Such statements are inadequate. What do "really understand" and "appreciate" mean? If the school leaders want to know whether the prospective voters are able to identify (or recite or list) the present sources of the school district's funds, the relative proportion (within given ranges) of the total revenues that is derived from each source, or the programs and services that have been suspended because of the level of existing levies, they should so specify. Terms such as identify, list, and recite are much less subject to a variety of interpretations than are words such as understand, appreciate, enjoy, and believe.

In summary, school leaders should insure that the purposes for a public opinion polling are defined (a) in enough detail to enable decisions to be made about the population to be polled, the questions to be asked, and the methods of data analysis, and (b) in words that are subject to only a limited number of interpretations. The publications by Mager[1] (although aimed at the development of instructional objectives) and Stephan and McCarthy[2] contain many ideas germane to defining purposes.

Choosing the Sample for the Poll

The basic idea of sampling is simple: To gain information about a given population, we examine some representative members of the population and extend the findings from those members to the whole population. Answers to three basic questions are needed in the sampling process. (1) What is the population? (2) How is the sample to be determined? (3) What size sample is desired?

Population Defined

Technically, population refers to all of a specified group of persons or objects; therefore, it is crucial that the group to be canvassed by a poll be precisely and clearly defined. Within a given school district there are innumerable population groups. For example, there is a registered voter group, a group with children currently enrolled in the schools of the district, a group of females who are registered voters and who are mothers or guardians of children currently enrolled in schools. Obviously, most of us belong to a vast number of different populations.

The definition of population should be consistent with the purposes of the polling. School leaders who want to know if they can expect a favorable vote on the increase in the school district's operating millage levy, should define the population to be sampled as all persons who are registered to vote in the district millage election. If the aim of the polling is to gather opinions on the practices of reporting about children's in-school progress to parents, the target population should be defined as all parents or legal guardians of pupils currently enrolled in the schools of the district.

Methods of Choosing the Sample

Once the population has been defined in terms that enable the pollster to determine whether a given person is to be included or excluded from the target group, the next decision to be made relates to the method to be used in choosing the sample. As previously indicated, the basic aim is to choose persons in a manner that enables the pollster to generalize about the total group (population). Obviously, errors in generalization due to sample bias can be avoided by a census — polling all members of the specified population. However, this is often impractical. Therefore, the following paragraphs con-

sider four basic methods of choosing a sample — random, systematic, stratified, and cluster.

Random Sampling. A random sample is a sample drawn in such a manner as to insure that each member of the target population has an equal chance of being included as a member of the sample each time a choice is made. No person is excluded except by chance. To illustrate, if the population is defined as all residents of the school district 21 years of age and over on a given date, and the sample is drawn from a list of registered voters of the district, those persons over 21 who had not registered to vote would be excluded by the choice of the voter list — not by chance. Moreover, if the voter list had not been recently "updated," some persons who have moved from the district would be included when they should have been excluded. (Note that if the target population is defined as "residents," an operational definition of the term resident must be provided. For example, are transients, such as students, salesmen, and members of the armed forces, currently living in the district, to be considered residents? Are persons who have some "ties" within the district by nature of property ownership, business ownership, or family but who are not actually living within the district to be considered residents?)

Mechanically there are several methods of drawing a random sample. Each method requires the numbering or other labeling of each entity within the target population. The most commonly used methods include drawing from a container that holds numbered slips or balls of equal size, using a table of random numbers, and using a computer-generated set of random numbers. The numbers on the slips or balls, of course, correspond to the numbers assigned to the entities within the population. The publications by Edwards[3] and Wallis and Roberts,[4] among others, contain tables of random numbers and directions for their use. Most statistical computer centers have "canned" programs to generate sets of randomly selected numbers. Use of the container method is not very practical for sampling large populations.

There are two major advantages to using the simple random method in drawing a sample. First, there is no need to have advance knowledge about relationships between various characteristics of the population and the phenomenon being investigated. Thus, for example, no advance investigation need be made of how factors like age, race, sex, and property ownership relate to voting behavior. Second,

if the sample drawn is of reasonable size, the "laws of probability" are such that it can usually be relied on to provide a representative cross-section of the population.

There are three major disadvantages to the simple random method. First, it is often difficult to secure a complete and up-to-date list of the entire target population. Second, if the sample to be chosen is quite small in relation to the population, the probability of a "poor" sample is increased. Third, the method can be time-consuming and expensive, in terms of both numbering or otherwise labeling each person in the population, and polling a sample that tends to be widely dispersed geographically.

Systematic Sampling. A systematic or "regular interval" sample is a sample drawn by using a list of the target population and including every 10th, 20th, 50th, or other interval of the entities to obtain the desired number in the sample. Suppose we decide to draw a sample of 100 individuals who belong to the Sunbright High School Parent-Teacher Association and there is available an alphabetical listing of the 1,000 members of that organization. First, 100 is divided into 1,000 to determine the interval size (in this example, 10). Second, the starting number (from 01 through 10 in this case) is selected by an approved random method. Third, assuming the starting number drawn in this case is 03, numbers 03, 13, 23, 33, and so on are selected until the sample of 100 is secured.

On occasion, polls have been taken by going into a defined geographic area such as a school district and interviewing in each nth household on each street. In essence, this is a systematic sample of households.

A systematic sample is often confused with a simple random sample. It is not a random sample, because once the starting number is chosen each entity does not have an equal chance of being included in the sample. A systematic sample requires less effort to draw than a random sample and in most instances leads to the same results — a representative cross-section of the population.

There is one major pitfall. A biased sample can result if the listing used is associated in some manner with the phenomenon being investigated. Suppose the school leaders wanted to estimate the average annual salary of the certified employees of the school district, and they used a listing of these employees in the order of their annual salaries (from high to low). If an interval of 10 were used and two samples were chosen with different starting numbers (02 in one in-

stance and 08 in the other, for example), marked differences in the average salary figure obtained could occur. This would be true particularly if the top executives in the district were few in number and their pay was considerably greater than the pay of other employees.

Except for this pitfall, the advantages and disadvantages of the systematic sampling method are similar to those for the simple random sample.

Stratified sampling. Stratified sampling involves the process of dividing the target population into a number of subpopulations (strata) and then selecting samples from within each stratum independently, most commonly using the random method. This technique is often referred to as stratified random sampling. (It is also possible to select from within the strata by the systematic method.) In most polling situations the number selected from within a stratum will be proportional to the size of the stratum in relation to the total target population. In the event school leaders prefer to draw a disproportional sample (i.e., oversampling within some strata and undersampling within others), this disproportion must be corrected mathematically to estimate the results for the total target population accurately. A disproportional sample might be used, for example, when some strata are so small that a proportional sample would be very small, thus increasing the chance of bias.

The relative advantages of stratified random sampling compared to simple random sampling have been the focus of considerable discussion among statisticians. A review of the literature on the subject leads to the following conclusions:

1. If there is no knowledge about the relationship between the characteristics of the target population and the phenomenon in question, stratified random sampling is probably no better than simple random sampling. On the other hand, if there is some known correlation, for example, between such factors as age, education, and income, and voting behavior for the target population, use of a stratified sampling procedure, using age, education, and income strata, is preferred in polling on voter preferences. (In effect this would enable the pollster to assess the voting preferences of several groups — the less than high school education group, the $10,000 or more annual income group, and the like — within the target population.)

2. If there are some extremely small strata (in relation to the total target population) and it is deemed essential that these be represented in the sample, the stratified method is preferred, because it is

possible to miss these strata in a straight random sample. For example, if it is desired to insure that the small black population of a district is proportionally represented, a stratified method should be used, particularly if a small sample is drawn.

3. The stratified method permits selection of different proportions from different subpopulations, if desired.

Cluster Sampling. Cluster sampling involves selecting clusters or groups of entities rather than individual entities as sampling units and then studying all or a sample of the entities within the selected clusters. For example, to poll male heads of households within a city, we might use city blocks as the sampling unit, select a given number of blocks at random, and then poll all or a sample (chosen by a random or systematic method) of the male householders within the blocks selected. The primary reason for using a cluster of entities (in this instance city blocks) as a sampling unit, is lack of a complete listing of the individual entities in the target population (in this instance male heads of households). Another reason might be to get a sample that is not as widely dispersed over the geographic area. Thus, cluster sampling is generally an easier and less expensive method for polling. However, it is generally conceded that the cluster method produces a larger sampling error than a stratified or random sample of equal size. The primary reason is that the clusters (city blocks, in the example used) may be composed of individual entities that are very homogeneous, thus reducing the representativeness of the total sample.

Considerations in Selecting a Sampling Method

Because of the variety of circumstances that might impinge upon any opinion polling effort, to suggest the best method of sampling would be presumptuous. However, generally the simple random sample is appropriate if (1) a complete listing of the target population is available, (2) there is no known relationship between population characteristics and the phenomenon being investigated, and (3) school leaders are willing to expend the necessary resources to number all entities in the population and contact the sample selected.

In some school elections, a series of polls may be taken as a basis for campaign strategy as well as to determine voter preference. In such cases, a stratified random or systematic sample may be preferred. This will enable the school leaders to determine the opinions

of the several subpopulations ("publics") within the voter group. When the same sample is used for each poll in the series, this is often referred to as panel sampling.

If no listing of the population is available, or the school leaders have limited resources to commit, clusters may be used as the sampling unit and individuals within the clusters may then be sampled.

There may be a few occasions when none of the four methods described is most feasible. For example, suppose that 5 voting precincts out of a total of 30 precincts in a given school district gave combined total yes-no votes in the last five annual school millage elections that were proportional to the yes-no vote for the total district. In such a case, school leaders might decide that a census (a poll of every voter) of the five precincts would be the best indicator of the vote for the total districts.

Another approach that was widely used at one time in nationwide opinion polls is referred to as quota sampling. It is based on the premise that the sample should contain individuals having certain characteristics in the same proportion as these characteristics exist in the target population. Therefore, using available data, such as United States census reports, the target population is divided into numerous mutually exclusive subpopulations (strata). The sample to be chosen is divided on a proportional basis among the several strata. Interviewers are then assigned the responsibility of selecting the defined number of persons within each stratum. The interviewer may be told, for example, how many females of a given age group, a given educational level, a given income level, and the like he must obtain. The interviewer is free to choose the respondents subject to the quota restrictions mentioned. The quota sampling procedure is similar to the stratified approach, but the critical difference stems from interviewer choices within each stratum. If the interviewer selects his respondents in random fashion then the technique is equivalent to a stratified random sample. However, interviewers often have specific habits that cause them not to select their respondents in random fashion. Stated another way, the basic problem in quota sampling is the lack of full control. Nevertheless, the quota method is often used to select respondents from within geographic clusters, such as city blocks.

Determining the Size of the Sample

In addition to deciding what method of sampling is to be used, school leaders are confronted with determining the size of the sample

to be drawn. A cursory review of the literature on the subject suggests the following generalizations:

1. The larger the target population the smaller the proportion of the population needed for an adequate sample.

2. The more homogeneous the population the smaller the sample needed.

3. The more heterogeneous the population the larger the sample needed, unless stratification is used to compensate for the heterogeneity.

4. If the aim is to sample persons and some other sampling unit is used (such as the city block) the sample needs to be relatively large.

5. With fairly large populations, merely increasing the sample size does not necessarily increase the accuracy. In one often cited study, it was found that sample sizes of 10 percent, 5 percent, 2.5 percent, and 2 percent were all substantially accurate when compared with the data gathered from the total population (approximately 12,000).[5]

The simple random sample, systematic sample, stratified random sample, and stratified systematic sample can be classified as essentially probability samples. There are mathematical methods of estimating the sample size needed when a probability sampling approach is used. To make this estimation the school leaders must decide the amount of variation that can be tolerated in the estimate and how much assurance they need that the estimate will fall within the variation limits established. In other words, how much probability do they want that the sample's distributions will not differ by more than plus or minus X points from the "true" distributions for the population.

To illustrate the mathematical calculation, assume we want to sample voter preference about a given issue in a school district, and we want the chances to be at least 90 in 100 that the distributions computed from our sample will not differ from the population distributions by more than plus or minus 5 percentage points. In this instance the variation we would tolerate is plus or minus 5 percentage points and the assurance we want that the results will be within that range of variation is 90 in 100 chances.

Assume also that the statistic we want is the percentage of voters who approve the measure. (Percentages are most often desired in opinion polling, but if averages are desired another formula is more appropriate.)

Assume that the target population consists of 10,000 individuals and that a simple random sample is to be drawn. To calculate the maximum sample size for the level of confidence desired, one suggested formula,[6] based on the chi-square statistic, is:

$$n = \frac{[X^2 N\Phi(1-\Phi)]}{[d^2(N-1)+X^2\Phi(1-\Phi)]}$$

where n = required sample size

X^2 = table value of chi-square for one degree of freedom and the desired confidence interval (90 percent is the confidence interval and the table value of X^2 is 2.706)

N = population size

Φ = the population proportion it is desired to estimate (.5 will give maximum sample size)

d = the degree of accuracy expressed as a proportion (.05 where ± 5 percent is the error that will be tolerated).

Substituting the figures from our example:

$$n = \frac{[2.706(10,000)\ (.5)\ (1-.5)]}{[(.05)^2(10,000-1)+2.706(.5)\ (1-.5)]}$$

$$n = \frac{6765.0}{25.674} = 264$$

If the population size were 100,000 and the same conditions were maintained, the sample size needed would be only 271. However, keeping the population at 10,000, if we demanded that the variation be within 2.5 percentage points, and that the estimate fall within these limits 95 out of 100 times, the X^2 value becomes 3.841 (1 degree of freedom at the .95 confidence interval), the d becomes .025, and the required sample size is 1332. The obvious point is that when the variation limits are reduced and the required degree of accuracy is increased, the needed sample size increases rapidly.

If a stratified sampling method is to be used and a formula such as the one shown is applied, the sample size for each stratum should be computed. The sample size for the total population is the sum of the samples for the strata.

Another approach to the problem of sample size and amount of error in the estimate is to compute the standard error of the estimate after the results of the poll are determined. The sample size is arbitrarily chosen — 10 percent, 5 percent, or some other percentage of the population. Then the standard error of the estimate formula is applied to the poll results, to determine how close they probably are to the true population distribution. To illustrate, assume that out of a sample of 1,000 voters, 400 voters responded favorably to proposition X. To determine the standard error of the estimate of the 40 percent favorable responses, the following formula for computing the standard error of the estimate of a percentage could be used:

$$\sigma p = \sqrt{\frac{p(100-p)}{n}}$$

where σp =   standard error of the percentage

p =   the percentage

n =   size of sample

Substituting, it is found that:

$$\sigma p = \sqrt{\frac{40(100-40)}{1000}} = \sqrt{\frac{2400}{1000}} = 1.55\%$$

What the standard error of the estimate of the percentage means, essentially, is that if the data are normally distributed chances are 2 out of 3 that the "true" percentage of the population favoring proposition X in the illustration lies somewhere between 41.55 percent and 38.45 percent (± one standard error), and that chances are 19 out of 20 that the "true" percentage lies somewhere between 43.2 percent and 36.9 percent (± two standard errors).

In brief, the three major points for school leaders in deciding how large a sample is needed in a polling effort are: (1) if the sample is properly drawn, its size need not be excessive; (2) if possible, the

educators should decide how much faith must be placed in the sample results and use this as the basis for calculating the size of the sample; and (3) if a percent of the population is arbitrarily chosen for the size of the sample, they can compute the error "after the fact."

Methods of Contact

A poorly drawn sample of inadequate size is a major source of error in opinion polling; however, even assuming that an adequate sampling procedure is used, the polling effort is futile if careful attention is not given to the data-gathering process. Grievous errors can result from the data-gathering mechanism as well as from sampling. Two major dimensions are involved — the method of contact and the form of the data-recording instrument.

For the method of contact, school leaders have three basic options — mail, personal interview, and telephone interview. The advantages and disadvantages of each of these options are briefly reviewed.

Mail Contact

Use of the mail obviously requires some type of questionnaire as the device for collecting the data. The major advantages of the mailed questionnaire are:

1. It enables the pollster to reach a large and geographically dispersed sample at a relatively low cost. The mailed questionnaire is the most economical option if no personal followup is made.

2. Through the mail, contact may be made with persons who might not otherwise be reached. In some homes and offices, particularly those of the very affluent sector of the population, an interviewer (in person or via phone) may have difficulty gaining access. However, the access that may be gained by means of the mailed questionnaire does not insure that the person to whom it is addressed will actually review and respond to it.

3. The mailed questionnaire provides anonymity in responding. Although this is often cited as an advantage, it has been argued that some persons hesitate to commit themselves in writing even anonymously. Therefore, the claimed advantage of anonymity is open to question.

4. Use of the mailed questionnaire insures that each respondent

receives the same questions phrased in the same way. Thus each respondent has the same "set," and the data yielded are more comparable. A related and often cited advantage is that the information obtained is not funneled through an interviewer's personality.

5. The mailed questionnaire eliminates the need for time-consuming and costly training of interviewers.

These advantages are effectively offset by an imposing set of major disadvantages:

1. The returns from a mailed questionnaire are often quite low. The percentage of returns varies widely, but in many instances it is less than 10 percent. Assuming the sample initially chosen is appropriate, the extent to which the returns are below 100 percent is the extent of possible bias. Many authorities have argued that, unless steps are taken to insure almost 100 percent returns, the mailed questionnaire is so subject to bias that it should never be used in opinion polling.

There are procedures that may be used to check on possible bias within the group responding to mailed questionnaires. One method is to compare the group of those who returned the questionnaire after the initial request with the groups responding after one and two followup appeals. If these intergroup comparisons reveal major differences, some selective factor is probably operating and there is in fact a bias. Another approach is to select a sample from the nonrespondent group, contact the sample by telephone or personal interview, and then compare the results obtained from this group with the results of the mailed questionnaire. Again, if the results do not correspond, a bias factor may well be operating.

2. Even though a sincere effort is made to make directions and questions easily understood, there is always the risk that the respondent may misinterpret or not understand a set of directions or questions. A related disadvantage is that the respondent must be able to read and write. This may be a major limitation if the sample is likely to contain a number of persons who do not meet these assumed requirements.

3. Many persons, even though willing to respond, are likely to delay answering questionnaires and subsequent followup appeals. Thus, the mailed questionnaire poll will be spread over a relatively long time period. Some persons who respond are unwilling to take the time to write complete answers. Many persons would rather talk than write. If the questionnaire is brief, this may not be a severe limitation.

4. There is no opportunity in the mailed questionnaire to gauge the intensity of the respondents' opinions as written. For example, to a question that demands a "yes" or "no" response, one respondent may answer "no" with great hesitation. Another individual may respond "no" with the feeling that the word does not adequately reflect the depth of his opposition to the issue raised. The pollster receiving the data has two "no" responses that in reality are not comparable, but he has no way of knowing this.

Personal Contact

The major advantages usually advanced for the personal interview as a method of contact are:

1. Generally a very high percentage of the sample responds. Assuming the interviewers are capable, the refusal rate is usually low, and if callbacks are made, eventually most of the persons in the sample are contacted and respond.

2. The personal interview provides an opportunity to establish a level of rapport that may result in responses that could not otherwise be obtained. Obviously, the rapport established is a function of the skill of the interviewer. However, if appropriate rapport can be established, the respondent may reply with more spontaneity and in greater depth than could be achieved by any other contact method. If the respondent does not understand the question, is not giving a complete response, or indicates particular sensitivity about a given question, the personal interviewer can explain the question further, ask followup questions for more information, or develop a better "set" for sensitive questions.

3. The personal interviewer can secure data from persons who could not complete a questionnaire — the disabled, the very aged, the illiterate, and others.

4. An opportunity is afforded to gauge the intensity of the opinions held by the respondent and to observe nonverbal behavior.

5. The interviewer can be sure that he is getting only the respondent's opinions, whereas in completing a questionnaire the respondent may obtain assistance from other persons.

The major limitations of the personal interview are:

1. It is a time-consuming process. The information actually desired may take five minutes of interviewing time. However, in traveling to and from the interview, developing the "setting" for these responses,

and closing the interview, many times this amount of time may be consumed. The necessary process of training and supervising interviewers is also time-consuming.

2. It is a costly approach when compared to other methods of contact. Costs for training and supervising interviewers, transportation to and from interviews, and interview time must be considered. The cost differential between the personal interview and other methods of contact may not be as great as claimed if the geographic area for a given interviewer is limited. Comparative costs of the mailed questionnaire or telephone interview approach also rise when a personal followup of nonrespondents is conducted to insure a representative sample.

3. The organization and control of the personal interview approach are relatively complex. Supervisory personnel as well as a team of interviewers are required. The hours of contact will be irregular if a cross-section of the population is being polled (many persons must be contacted at night).

4. The presence of the interviewer may bias the respondent's reply. The interviewer may subconsciously ask questions in a leading manner or reveal his own biases. And some persons may hesitate to express opinions that deviate from the expected norm. For example, few people may be openly negative on questions relating to school improvement. Obviously, well-chosen, well-trained interviewers using a well-developed interview guide can help counteract this apparent limitation.

Telephone Contact

The third basic method of contact open to school leaders is the telephone. The major advantages of the telephone interview are:

1. In terms of achieving completed interviews, it is economical. A small number of well-trained interviewers operating from a single location can contact many persons spread over a wide geographic area for a relative low cost per completed contact. Compared with the personal interview, it provides an obvious saving in transportation costs and interviewer time costs. Some authorities claim it is more economical per return than the mailed questionnaire, particularly if followup procedures are used with the mailed questionnaire.

2. The telephone interview approach is quick. Polling need not extend over weeks as is the case with the mailed questionnaire. A

single telephone interviewer can conduct ten or more interviews in the time it takes a personal interviewer to conduct one.

3. Assuming the interviewers are capable, the refusal rate among persons successfully contacted is low. Some authorities suggest that 3 percent or fewer refusals are to be expected. When the telephone approach is used, loss in sample occurs mainly from unanswered and busy telephones — not refusals.

4. The organization and control of the polling is relatively simple. Assuming the interviewers function from a single location, interviewer errors can be quickly identified and corrected by supervisors, questions can be handled on the spot, and a ready supply of names can be kept available to each interviewer.

The major disadvantages of the telephone interview are:

1. It is likely to result in a biased sample if a representative group of parents, voters, or the like is desired. For example, certain socioeconomic groups tend to have telephones with greater frequency than others, homeowners tend to have telephones in greater proportion than renters, and women tend to answer telephones more often than men. Therefore, the telephone interview approach may be limited in usefulness to polls covering a population that is likely to consist of 100 percent telephone subscribers (e.g., middle and upper socioeconomic class families).

2. There is no opportunity to observe nonverbal behavior and characteristics of the respondent. For example, the respondent may be antagonized by a given question or by the total interview situation and deliberately "fake" responses. The telephone interviewer does not have the opportunity to evaluate such a situation. If characteristic data, such as sex, age estimate, and race, are sought, these questions must be asked, because there is no opportunity to observe them.

3. Because the telephone interview must be relatively brief, the situation is not conducive to soliciting detailed opinions, asking probing and followup questions, and receiving amplification of responses.

4. Because it is relatively difficult to establish the credentials of interviewers by telephone and the opportunity for developing rapport is limited, respondents may be somewhat guarded in the opinions expressed.

Data-Recording Instruments

Regardless of the method of contact selected, a well-developed instrument to guide the questioning and record responses is essential. When used in the telephone or personal interview situation, the instrument is usually referred to as an interview guide or schedule. In mail contact, the term used is questionnaire. Some prefer to limit use of the term questionnaire to a mailed instrument designed to elicit factual information and to use the term "opinionnaire" for a mailed instrument designed to secure opinions.

At the present time, development of interview schedules and questionnaires is more an art than a science. In fact, some persons successful in developing such instruments for opinion polling have stated this bluntly. Nevertheless, there are a number of points in instrument development on which there is general agreement.

Types of Items

The instrument, whether it is a mailed questionnaire or an interview guide, generally consists of three types of items: identifying items, items about the respondent's personal characteristics, and items relating to the subject of the poll. The amount of identifying information obviously varies with the nature of the poll. Usually it is essential to include items that enable the completed instrument to be associated with a given respondent or subgroup of respondents. This facilitates checking omissions and determining whether a given person has responded. This may be as simple as a name and address or identification by voting precinct. If the responses are to be analyzed by data processing equipment, a numerical coding system is suggested. For example, if a random sample of the registered voter population of a given school district is used, each person on the voter list is assigned a 6-digit number (000001–999999). For a fuller identification, a 12-digit field might be used — two digits for the school district or poll identification, two digits for the interviewer, two digits for voting precinct, and six digits identifying the individual respondent (corresponding to the number assigned on the voter list). The code can be inserted before mailing the questionnaire or assigning an interviewer or it can be inserted when the questionnaire is returned (assuming the respondent provides the necessary information) or by the interviewer on the spot.

The items concerning personal characteristics should be determined by consideration of (a) any perceived relevance between selected personal characteristics and opinions on the issue being polled, and (b) the subgroup comparisons that will eventually be desired (e.g., comparisons between age groups). Some of the items that might be used are age, sex, marital status, education, birthplace, political party affiliation, race or ethnic group, occupation, family or household size, number or ages of children in school, income, and house occupancy status (owner or renter). For brevity, school leaders should avoid including personal characteristics items that correlate highly with one another (e.g., income and education).

The items on the subject being considered in the poll are discussed in detail below.

Wording of Items

In wording items, it is generally agreed that (a) "double-barreled" items should be avoided, (b) ambiguous items should be avoided, (c) leading questions should be avoided, (d) items should be concise, (e) items should be asked in language that the respondents can understand, and (f) emotion-laded words should be avoided. A double-barreled item is one that contains an implicit assumption about the respondent or the response or includes two or more questions. For example, "How long does it take you to read your daily newspaper?" carries with it the assumption that the respondent reads a daily newspaper. A preliminary question to determine whether a paper is read should be used. Another example: "I favor higher salaries for teachers and think taxes should be increased for this purpose." Some persons may agree with the total statement. Others might favor higher teachers' salaries but not higher taxes. In summary, as a general rule, one item should never be used when two could be used. This is a bit of an overstatement, but it is a good guideline.

A leading item is one that suggests an answer. An ambiguous item is one that the respondent can easily misinterpret. It may be impossible to design items that are unambiguous for everyone but the effort should be made. A single example illustrates an ambiguous and leading item with emotion-laden wording: "Don't you think hippies should be dealt with firmly?" Ambiguities abound — the term "hippies" is subject to many definitions; the term "firmly" means different things to people; and if the respondent answers "yes," he could

mean, "Yes, I don't think hippies should be dealt with firmly," or, "Yes, I do think hippies should be dealt with firmly." The phrase, "Don't you think," tends to lead the respondent in a given direction. Also, for many, "hippie" is an emotion-laden term.

If an item is long and complex, particularly if it is presented by an interviewer, the respondent may become confused and the subsequent response may not be an accurate reflection of his opinion. There may be instances in which long and explanatory items are necessary. If so, in a personal interview situation, it is probably advantageous to have the item printed on a card for the respondent to read. The use of concise questions in a telephone interview is almost a "must" because it is impossible to present the respondent with a printed statement.

Constructing items in familiar language is a difficult guideline to achieve. Generally, the language used in schedule or questionnaire items should be geared to the least intelligent and least educated segment of the sample to be polled. Readability formulas are readily available to determine the language level of items to insure that the desired level is achieved. However, language designed for the least intelligent and educated respondents may be viewed as condescending and offensive by the more intelligent and highly educated segments of the sample. Also, certain words are familiar to some socioeconomic groups and some geographic sectors of the country and not to others. For example, the term "beat" is commonly used in certain sectors of the United States to describe what persons in other sectors refer to as a civil district within a county governmental unit.

Emotion-laden words are those that tend to arouse a person and cause him to react without thought to the context in which the word is used. Words that are emotion-laden obviously differ with the person and the times. In recent years, such words as liberal, conservative, civil rights, big business, Red, union, big government, and race could be classified as emotion-laden. Also, names of public figures often arouse emotions. Careful scrutiny of the words used and elimination of those thought to have high emotional content are valuable.

Instrument Tryout

The best means of insuring that the items used in an interview schedule or questionnaire are clear, concise, and easily understood is to conduct an instrument tryout or pilot run. After the data-gather-

ing instrument has been refined to the satisfaction of the persons responsible for its development, a small sample (10 to 40 persons) that will not be a part of the sample used in the polling but that is from the same population should be drawn. Each of the selected persons should be interviewed or sent the questionnaire in the manner planned for the polling activity, except that a followup should be conducted (by personal interview, if possible) to discuss the respondent's understanding of each item. The instrument should be revised as dictated by the feedback received. If the feedback indicates that numerous items and directions are in need of revision, a second pilot run is desirable.

Items to be Included

Since brevity in an interview or questionnaire is desirable, another major point on which there appears to be general agreement is that the data-gathering instrument should contain only items for information that cannot be obtained from other sources (i.e., voting records, city directories, and the like) and items that are essential to the subject of the polling. The exception is that it is probably desirable to include one or more items designed to verify or check the consistency of the responses. For example, an item on property ownership or whether the respondent voted in the last millage election might be included and the response "checked" against the appropriate public records. Another approach would be to include two opinion items about the same phenomenon but stated in slightly different form and spaced rather far apart. If a cross-check shows that the respondent has not been truthful or consistent, his other responses might be appropriately discarded.

Other Considerations

There are several other considerations in instrument construction about which school leaders must make decisions. Since the authorities are not in general agreement about what is "best practice," school leaders must evaluate the pros and cons and their own situations as a basis for decisionmaking. These considerations include: (a) how much structure to provide the respondent, (b) how to arrange the items within the instrument, (c) whether to use disguised items, (d) how to handle sensitive items, and (3) what physical form the instrument should take.

Structure of Items. It is generally accepted, in opinion polling, that each respondent has to be provided the same "set," to the extent possible. Therefore, in an interview situation, directions and questions should be provided in the same manner and order to each person interviewed. Some authorities would allow the interviewer to modify the language slightly to "fit" the respondent. Others would reject even slight language modifications.

A more basic decision relates to the form of the items. Two options are available to the pollster: open-end items and closed-end items. An open-end item is phrased in a manner that allows great latitude in responding. Examples are:

What do you think of the way the local school leaders spend the money made available for the schools?

What do you think about a real property tax increase for schools?

React to the following statement: The local school district leaders have been using school building funds unwisely.

Closed-end items are of three basic types — dichotomous questions or statements, multiple choice questions or statements, and ranking questions or statements. Examples of dichotomous items are:

Do you read a local newspaper?
     Yes   No
Citizens should be informed about how the tax dollar is spent.
     Yes   No

Examples of multiple choice items are:

How long have you lived in Zach Township?
     Less than 5 years
     5–10 years
     More than 10 years
On the whole, Zach Township School District is
     ☐ An outstanding school district
     ☐ A good school district
     ☐ A fair school district
     ☐ A poor school district
(Check the response that best describes your opinion.)

Examples of ranking items are:

Following are several sources of information about the local schools. Place a 1 by the source from which you receive the most information, a 2 by the source from which you receive the next most information, etc.

☐ Neighbors
☐ Your children
☐ Relatives (other than children)
☐ Coworkers
☐ Local newspaper
☐ School district employees
☐ School district publication
☐ Local radio
☐ Local television

How important are the following characteristics of a good tax? Place a 1 by the most important, a 2 by the next most important, etc.
☐ Easy to collect
☐ Each pays in accord with his ability
☐ Predictable in terms of income it will produce
☐ Those who benefit will pay

The major advantage of the open-end item is that because the structure is loose the respondent may provide more information and in greater depth than if the item had a series of fixed alternative responses. Because open-end items lead to a wide variety of responses, the major shortcoming of this approach is the time-consuming process of making an "after the fact" classification system and analyzing the responses according to that system. Also, some writers argue that when the mailed questionnaire is used, many people will not take the time to write complete responses to open-end items. Thus, the closed-end item has the advantages of being relatively quick and "clean" to analyze and less time-consuming for a questionnaire respondent.

The means of analysis should be kept in mind when developing alternatives for closed-end items. For example, if age data are sought and the sample will be broken into only three age categories, these categories should be the alternatives offered to the respondents.

Arrangement of Items. In organizing the instrument, most authorities state that the items should be arranged logically for respondent understanding. This means that (a) items should be arranged by topic, (b) general items should precede specific items, (c) simple items should precede complex items, (d) appealing items should precede less appealing items, and (e) items that have the same directions for responding should be grouped together. However, on many occasions it is not possible to follow guidelines (a) through (d) and also group items according to directions for responding. Thus, a priority among guidelines must be established. The authors suggest that if the

directions are complex guideline (e) should be given the higher priority; otherwise, in cases of conflict, the other guidelines should be given the higher priority.

Disguised Items. Since in our culture many persons hesitate to respond in a manner that deviates from the norm, particularly when asked about education and its value, several techniques have been developed to disguise the real purpose of the inquiry, in both open-end and closed-end items. These techniques include word association, sentence completion, story construction, judgment tests, the semantic differential, and the slantwise question. The extent to which disguised items should be used in school election polls is certainly debatable. Due to technical considerations, the author's position is that most school district opinion polling efforts should avoid disguised items, except for the slantwise question (e.g., instead of asking a person directly how he will vote in an upcoming millage election, ask, "Is the school board's millage proposal reasonable?"). If some of the disguised techniques appear appropriate, expert assistance should be sought. For the interested reader, Sax provides an excellent review of disguised item techniques.[7]

Sensitive Items. Most polls include one or more sensitive items (i.e., items likely to arouse emotion or embarrass the respondent). Therefore, brief attention is given to suggestions about such items. In organizing the data-recording instrument, sensitive items should be interspersed with more neutral items and should not be placed at the beginning or end of the questionnaire or interview guide. The items could be slightly disguised in an advice-seeking form. For example, instead of, "What would induce you to favor higher taxes for schools?" use, "What do you feel school leadership could do to make the need for funds outweigh the need to keep taxes down?"

In the 1968 presidential campaign, one national polling group found that the support of a particular candidate increased approximately two percent (over the responses given directly to the interviewers) when the interviewers gave the respondents a "ballot" and asked them to mark the ballot and drop it in the "ballot box" they carried. The candidate in question was viewed as supporting many ideas that were in opposition to prevailing social concerns. Presumably, respondents were embarrassed to express support in face-to-face interviews. This technique may have merit if respondents are being asked directly in a personal interview situation how they will vote on a given school issue. Many persons apparently feel that it is not

"socially acceptable" to oppose the improvement of educational opportunities.

If an item is likely to embarrass a respondent because he lacks information, an explanation might be given preceding the question. For example, "There are two prevailing opinions on the issue. One point of view holds. . . ." Another example: "A bond referendum has been called for June of this year. You'll be asked to vote for or against the issuing of $20,000,000 for constructing new schools in Brentwood, Eva, Hillsdale, and York." Then ask the question. If explanatory items are used, the explanation should be clearly separated from the question on the questionnaire or by the interviewer. If the explanation is long and complex, the interviewer may well give it to the respondent in writing to follow as he presents it orally.

Physical Form. If the interview is the method of contact, the physical form of the interview guide assumes importance primarily for data-recording and analysis purposes. If the items are almost exclusively closed-end, a reusable guide and a separate response-recording form for each respondent is probably appropriate. The reusable guide should be of heavy, high-quality paper, of a size that is easily handled by the interviewer, printed on one side only, with the items well spaced and printed in large type. If complex or explanatory items are included, they should be printed on separate cards that can be presented to respondents. The response-recording forms should be arranged so that the interviewer can record quickly (by O, X, √, or brief code) and easily follow the form in recording. If the responses are to be keypunched for data processing equipment directly from the response-recording form, it is probably advisable to arrange the items in vertical columns, indicate the card columns in which the response is to be punched, and use only a numerical code. The physical form of the instrument should be checked by the data processing personnel before its use. Corrections made by them can save many hours and dollars.

If numerous open-end items are to be used, the reusable interview guide is inappropriate. The recording should be done directly on the guide, and its physical structure should allow the interviewer to do this quickly and fully.

If the personal interview method of contact is used, the interviewers should also be provided with an identification badge and a letter, signed by the official responsible for the poll, that introduces the interviewer, states the purpose of the polling, and identifies the sponsoring organization.

If the mailed questionnaire method of contact is used, the physical form of the instrument is important not only for recording and analysis but for "selling" the respondent on participating in the polling effort. Consideration should be given to size, quality of paper, color of paper, item spacing, and method of reproduction. The standard 8½" x 11" questionnaire is often used; it fits well in an envelope, is easily handled, and fits most files. For very long questionnaires, a booklet that will fit the standard number 10 envelope may be used. This may arouse respondent interest and be easily mailed, but it is difficult to handle for data analysis. For very short questionnaires, a double post card is often used. Half of the card contains directions and explains the purpose of the polling; the other half is the questionnaire, which can be torn off and returned.

Durable, high-quality paper is necessary if the questionnaire is to be printed or handled a great deal. Paper color has been a topic of discussion among some pollsters. Prevailing opinion holds that light, subdued colors are preferable. It is important to provide enough space between items for the respondent to answer the questions and to avoid the appearance of being cluttered or complicated. The commonly used methods of reproduction are spirit duplicating (Dittoing), mimeographing, offset printing, and letterpress printing. The latter two are more expensive for a small number of questionnaires, but in appearance they are superior and preferred.

A person who has often been polled by questionnaire summed up the importance of physical form as follows: "If I get a questionnaire and it appears that considerable time, effort, and expense went into its development, I assume it is important enough for me to complete." Obviously, any mailed questionnaire should contain a stamped, self-addressed envelope (or post card) for its return, and a cover letter. The cover letter should explain the purpose of the poll, identify the sponsoring organization, request the respondent's cooperation, give an estimate of the time required to complete the questionnaire, and set a date of requested return.

Organizing and Conducting the Poll

Obviously, one person must be charged with leading the total effort and fixing the responsibilities of each person involved in a poll. The task of organizing and conducting an opinion poll is a function of (a) the size of the sample, (b) the method of contact, and (c) the

extent of data analysis. For example, polling 200 or 300 persons by means of a mailed one-page questionnaire might require the services of one or two professionals and a like number of clerks on a part-time basis; polling roughly 1,000 persons in a large geographic area by means of personal interview on three different occasions might require 40 or more persons working part and full-time for several weeks. In the first instance, organization is a simple matter; in the latter it is much more complex.

In most situations it is probably advantageous to use some management technique such as PERT (Program Evaluation and Review Technique)[8] as an aid in organizing and conducting the project. These techniques require that the activities in the project be identified and detailed, that relations of one to another be examined to determine if activities can be conducted concurrently or if one is dependent on completion of others, and that time estimates be made for each activity and the total project.

Time

One of the first considerations in organizing and conducting an opinion poll is time. Two dimensions are involved — the time required from inception (decision to conduct the poll) to completion (a written report in the hands of school leaders), and time of completion in relation to a scheduled event (e.g., the date of a school bond referendum).

Assume for example, that the school officials in a local district desire to conduct a series of three opinion polls among the registered voters within the school district in relation to an upcoming school construction bond referendum. Broadly stated, their purposes are to determine if the registered voter group and selected subgroups can identify the school building proposals of the district, whether they are positively or negatively inclined toward the proposals, the means by which they have been receiving information about the district, and their voting preference on the bond referendum. With such purposes, the school leaders obviously want to use the data as a basis for campaign strategy. A type of probability sample is selected, and contact by personal interview is chosen.

The school leaders must decide completion dates for the polls in relation to the scheduled referendum. If the first poll is to be used as a basis for deciding what means of communication will be used, what groups must be informed, and what information must be communi-

cated, they may want the poll completed four months before the
referendum. If the second poll is to ascertain how well the campaign
is going and to determine what changes in tactics are needed, they
may want the second poll completed one month before the referendum. If the third is to provide a basis for a concerted effort with
groups who are undecided or tend to be negative and for holding
efforts with the positive groups, they may want the last poll to be
completed ten days or sooner before the referendum.

In determining the time required from inception to completion of
each poll, consideration must be given to the time required to (a)
define the specific purposes for the poll, (b) develop the interview
guide, (c) secure interviewers, (d) train interviewers, (e) try out and
revise the interview guide, (f) reproduce the interview guide, (g) determine the sampling procedure, (h) select the sample, (i) provide
publicity, (j) collect the data (conduct the interviews), (k) prepare
the data for analysis, (l) analyze the data, and (m) prepare the report.
Obviously, several of these activities can be conducted concurrently.
Many of these activities were discussed previously. In the paragraphs
that follow, attention is given to the others — securing, training, and
supervising interviewers, publicity, and data analysis. Obviously, if a
mailed questionnaire is the method of contact, interviewer procure-
ment, training, and supervision are not required.

Securing Interviewers

In securing interviewers, it is necessary to decide what characteristics they should possess. Writers have suggested that interviewers
should (a) have the ability to converse easily with persons from a
variety of social, ethnic, and economic backgrounds, (b) have the
ability to ask questions without indication of bias, (c) possess the
patience to listen to respondents, (d) have an appealing personality,
(e) be able to understand and follow instructions precisely, (f) be
capable of observing detail and quickly sizing up situations, (g) have
the ability to comprehend and objectively and legibly record information received, (h) be persistent and not easily discouraged by re-
buffs, (i) be free to work odd hours, (j) be able to read a map or be
thoroughly familiar with the geographic area, and (k) have access to
an automobile and the ability to drive it. The last two factors mentioned become important if the interviewers' assignments will be
widespread geographically in areas without adequate public transpor-

tation. In opinion polling about school matters, the authors believe that both male and female interviewers can be used and that age is not a significant factor. Also, the interviewers should not be well acquainted with the persons whom they will interview or closely identified with the school district. Thus, parent-teacher organization members, members of a Citizens for Better Schools committee, school election campaign workers, and off-duty school employees should not be used as interviewers.

In determining the number of interviewers needed, four basic factors should be kept in mind: (1) How much information is being sought from the respondents and how long will it take to secure it in an interview situation? (2) How widespread geographically are the assignments for a given interviewer? (3) Is a particular person to be interviewed or will any person in a given household be acceptable? (4) How much total time has been allowed to complete the interviewing phase of the polling?

To illustrate, in one polling effort conducted by one of the authors, the time required to secure the data from a respondent averaged about 20 minutes. The assignments for each interviewer were concentrated in a few city blocks, and any responsible adult in a selected household could be interviewed. In this situation, it was found that 15-20 interviews per day were completed. However, in another poll where the time required to secure the needed data also averaged about 20 minutes, the interviewers completed only 5-7 interviews per day, because the respondents were spread throughout the civil district of a county and a specified person had to be interviewed.

The sources from which interviewers may be secured will vary from school district to school district. Among the groups often used are housewives (who may be secured through local employment agencies or a newspaper ad), college students, college students' and staff members' wives, high school students (their use in polls involving sensitive items is questionable), retired but still active persons, and persons who have had previous polling and interviewing experience (e.g., U.S. census workers). Some polls have been conducted using volunteer interviewers from local civic clubs. The authors' experience with such interviewers has not been very satisfactory, since they are often selected by the sponsoring club and may or may not be capable and dedicated to the task.

Training and Supervising Interviewers

The training of interviewers should include (a) informing them about the purposes of the poll and how the information will be tabulated and used, (b) informing them about the sampling procedure and the need to follow it exactly, (c) reviewing basic considerations in interviewing (e.g., introductory comments, how to deal with reluctant respondents), (d) carefully reviewing the interview guide and instructions (including explicit instructions on how to record data), (e) enacting a demonstration interview, (f) having the interviewers "interview" each other, (g) having each interviewer interview at least one person from the population under consideration who will not be included in the sample, and (h) providing detailed information on "mechanics" (i.e., pay, to whom they are responsible, to whom they should refer questions, when interviews are to be completed, where completed guides are to be returned, and the like). If the polling involves 15 or fewer interviewers, the training may well be accomplished in 1½ days, and might be organized as follows: morning of first day — presentation of verbal instructions, review of guides and procedures, and demonstration interview; afternoon of first day — interviewers interviewing each other and follow-up discussion; morning of second day — trial interview in the field, follow-up discussion, and distribution of interviewing assignments (including means of locating assignments).

In supervising interviewers, five guidelines are suggested:

1. Each interviewer should have a single supervisor to whom he is responsible.

2. An early check should be made of the work of each interviewer, so that errors are discovered and corrected.

3. Each interviewer should be given a reasonable daily or weekly quota.

4. Each completed and returned interview guide should be immediately checked for completeness and to ascertain whether recording instructions are being followed.

5. Throughout the interviewing period spot checks of each interviewer's work should be conducted to insure that the data submitted are accurate.

Publicity

The American public today is reasonably knowledgeable about opinion polling. Nevertheless, publicity and good public relations will enhance the polling effort. Some days before the polling actually occurs, by means of newspaper, radio, and television releases, the public can be informed that the polling will occur, why it is being done, who will be polled, the kinds of questions that will be asked, how the interviewers may be identified, and how the information will be used. Also, public endorsement of the effort by locally prominent persons and groups can be most helpful in securing cooperation. As the polling progresses, periodic releases noting progress and problems, expressing appreciation for cooperation, and restating the purposes and procedures are suggested. Immediately after the polling has been completed, it is a good idea to have "wrap-up" releases and statements that essentially are expressions of appreciation from prominent persons and groups as well as the sponsoring agency.

Data Analysis

The primary approach to analyzing data secured in an opinion poll is to determine frequency and percentage distributions, medians, means, and standard deviations for the sample and make estimates for the target population. The analyzed data are then presented in table, graph, and narrative form. Generally, the opinion data are analyzed by subgroups of the sample group, based on personal characteristics of the respondents — age, sex, place of residence, occupation, and the like. However, in many instances it may be desirable to solicit a positive or negative response to key items and analyze the personal characteristics of these two "groups" of respondents. Such an analysis will identify and describe the segments of the public that are opposed and that are supportive of the proposal. In turn, this information can be used in planning election strategies.

When the subgroup analyses are completed, it may be desirable to make selected comparisons among subgroups using such simple statistical tools as rank order correlations, chi-square, or nonparametric significance of difference techniques (e.g., Mann-Whitney U Test or Kruskal-Wallis H Test).[9] As the authors have emphasized previously, the exact means of analysis should be considered from the outset of the polling effort (i.e., in defining purposes, selecting the sample, and developing the data-gathering instrument).

After the data have been tabulated and analyzed according to plan and the appropriate tables and graphs developed, the synthesized data should be carefully reviewed with questions such as the following in mind:

1. What are the agreements and differences in opinions among the subgroups?

2. What overall trends are evident?

3. To what extent do the data support or conflict with what was expected?

4. Are there patterns of responses that appear to defy logical explanation?

5. What is suggested for further action?

The answers to these questions frequently lead to further analysis both within and among subgroups and to the development of new subgroups for purposes of detailed analysis. Needless to say, the process of carefully and fully "teasing" the data will be greatly impaired if data processing equipment has not been used to prepare the data for analysis.

Using Poll Data in School Elections

The major justification for spending the time, money, and effort to conduct polls is to provide a basis for responding effectively to the various pressures and interests present among the several "publics" of the school district. Stated another way, if the data obtained from polls are not used by school leaders in deciding on election strategies, there is little justification for conducting polls. Thus, the key question at this point is: How do school leaders use poll data in school election campaigns? When we consider the myriad circumstances that are likely to be present in a given school election, to offer a precise blueprint for the use of data from polls would be fallacious. However, an example may be used to illustrate several ways that data from polls can be used.

A poll, conducted by the authors, was requested by the leaders of a school district (a) to aid them in deciding whether the timing was right to request a bond referendum for construction of school buildings, and (b) if they decided to request the referendum, to provide a basis for campaign strategy. The poll was conducted to determine for the total voter group and several "publics" within it (based on such factors as parental status, age, education, length of residence in the

district, occupation, property ownership, race, sex, and voting precinct) their (a) sources of information about the school district, (b) likes and dislikes about the school district, (c) suggestions for improvements within the district, (d) knowledge of school building conditions within the district, (e) knowledge of a possible school bond election, and (f) voting preference if a bond election was held. Using a recent registered voter list, a sample was drawn by voting precincts, selecting every nth person from each precinct list (a stratified systematic sample). A small alternate sample was also chosen in the same manner. The sample was of sufficient size to insure a 9 out of 10 chance that the percentage distributions obtained would be within ± 5 percentage points of the voter population distributions. Each person in the sample was contacted by personal interview. The interview guide used contained 20 items — 4 open-end and 16 closed-end.

Among the more significant findings and generalizations, based on an analysis of the data, were the following:

1. For the total group sampled (a) children, neighbors, school district employees, and one of the local newspapers were the major sources of information about the district; (b) administrative efforts to improve educational services and the extracurricular programs drew the greatest number of favorable comments; (c) the most frequently mentioned dislikes related to the qualifications of the teaching staff, some administrative practices, certain curriculum features, and facilities; (d) the most frequently mentioned suggestions for improvement concerned how to secure and hold better teachers and how to improve several aspects of the curriculum; (e) less than one-third of the sample displayed any real knowledge of the present conditions of the school buildings or had any knowledge of a possible school bond election; (f) over one-third of those sampled felt that some effort to secure new buildings should be made and roughly one-third were "concerned" but had no opinion about what should be done; and (g) roughly 30 percent of the group indicated they would vote for the bonds, about 10 percent indicated they would definitely vote against the bonds, and the rest were "undecided." Also, over half of those who were definitely opposed to the bond issue indicated that their major source of school information was the local newspaper previously mentioned.

2. When the parent group was compared to the nonparent group, three areas were found in which the responses of the two groups

were significantly different: (1) a much higher percentage of the parent group received most of their school information from children, (2) the parent group was far more interested in having new school buildings, and (3) a greater percentage of the parents indicated that they would vote "yes" on the bond issue.

3. When the white voter group and the nonwhite voter group were compared, their responses were significantly different in three areas: (1) the nonwhite group tended to rely far more frequently on newspapers and children for information about the school district, (2) the nonwhite group was far more supportive of new buildings than the white group, and (3) the nonwhite group had more dislikes and suggestions about staff and curriculum.

4. When the property-owning group was compared to the group of those who did not own property, there were two areas in which their responses were significantly different: (1) the property-owning group was less satisfied with the type of information received about the schools, and (2) the property-owning group indicated more frequently that they would vote "yes" in a school bond election.

5. When the group of voters who indicated that they would vote for the bond issue was compared to the group who said they would vote against the bond issue, it was found that the group supporting the bond issue (a) contained more parents, (b) depended to a much greater extent on neighbors and children for information, (c) had fewer long-term residents of the district, (d) was younger in age, (e) had a greater proportion of nonwhites, (f) had a greater proportion of females, (g) had more property owners, and (h) was concentrated in particular geographic sectors of the district. (The opposition was concentrated in two separate geographic sectors and was generally negative toward the district and its operation. The negative opinions that characterized these two sectors appeared to represent a reaction to the location of previously constructed buildings.)

6. Except as noted, the differences in responses of selected subgroups were insignificant.

Based on the poll, what suggestions for action could be offered to the leadership of the district — in what ways could the findings be used? There were several general indications that a bond referendum could be successful if the campaign strategy was carefully planned and diligently executed. However, it would probably be a close election. The generalization that the referendum could be successful seems justified in light of (a) the number of positively "leaning"

persons, (b) the number of persons with ambivalent opinions (the cross-pressured), and (c) the relatively small size of the hard core opposition. The generalization that such an election would be close is based on the fact that many persons had concerns and complaints relative to some aspects of the district's operation.

At a more specific level, the following suggestions for campaign tactics illustrate how the results of a poll can be used.

1. To the extent possible (considering the goals of the district, the resources available, the professional values of the school officials, and the ethical questions involved) take action to implement the suggestions offered by respondents and to correct conditions creating the dislikes mentioned by them regarding specific administrative practices and curriculum features. Particular attention should be paid to the suggestions and dislikes of the parent group, the "young in age" group, the property-owning group, the nonwhite group, and the group of relative newcomers to the district, because the data indicated a broad base of potential support among these groups. Also, every effort should be made to communicate to the "publics" the steps that are being taken.

2. Form a large, broadly representative, ad hoc committee to study the personnel practices relating to teaching staff and to offer recommendations for securing and holding better teachers. (This was a major area of expressed concern.)

3. Recruit, organize, and fully inform campaign workers in each district. In selecting campaign workers, make a deliberate effort to secure broad representation from among the young in age, nonwhite, and relative newcomer groups. (The data indicated that these groups were generally supportive.)

4. Insure that all employees of the school district are fully informed about the district's operations, its efforts to improve educational services, and the conditions related to the proposed bond issue. (The employees were a major source of information about the schools. If the employees do not understand the reasoning behind the request for bonds or are not convinced of the need for new school buildings, this fact alone might well bring about a defeat at the polls.)

5. In conveying information to the several "publics" about the efforts being made to improve and the condition of school buildings within the district, concentrate on (a) sending information, *not propaganda*, into the homes by children; (b) making presentations at

parent-teacher groups, civic and service clubs, neighborhood coffees, and the like; and (c) securing full and objective coverage in the widely-read local newspaper. (These were the extensively used sources of information — children, neighbors, and a local newspaper.) Consideration should also be given to using district administrators in group meetings. (The data indicated that their efforts were positively perceived.)

6. In view of the fact that (a) over half of the "definitely opposed" group listed the local newspaper as their major source of school information, and (b) the nonwhite group, which identified many dislikes and offered numerous suggestions, relied heavily on the newspaper for information, take care to work with the leadership of the local newspaper. Make an effort to secure editorial support and fair coverage.

7. For those precincts in the two geographic sectors where major opposition was concentrated, use a "soft sell" approach, and take care not to engage in activities that would encourage a major, active campaign on the part of these groups. An effort might be made to communicate the reasoning behind the decisions about previous building locations, but pressure that might lead to an adverse reaction should not be applied. (Several specific suggestions about dealing with the hard core opposition are offered in Chapter 5.)

8. In developing campaign literature, identify the school building needs exactly and clearly. (There was a general lack of this knowledge among the voters.) Specify these needs within the context of improving educational opportunities for children, however. (Buildings represented only one of the concerns of voters.)

9. In view of the broad base of potential support among the nonwhite, parent, young, and newcomer groups, make every effort to encourage persons in these groups to register to vote and to get them to the polls on election day.

The data from the poll could be used in other ways in the school election campaign. The ideas advanced here should suggest how poll data can be used to aid in (a) making a decision about requesting an election, (b) identifying and responding to the interests and concerns of the several "publics," (c) deciding on communication techniques, (d) identifying areas of potential support and opposition, (e) identifying the kind of information that should be communicated to the voters, and (f) identifying steps that might be quickly and reasonably undertaken to create a more favorable climate among the voters.

Again, the authors would remind the reader that data from public opinion polls are but one source of feedback. Therefore, the decision to act on the basis of poll data should be evaluated within the context of other types of feedback (e.g., feedback from community influentials).

Number, Costs, and Value of Polls

Predicated on the conviction that opinion polling is a major feedback process and, as such, an essential ingredient in successful school election campaigns, the authors have presented material designed to acquaint school leaders with the essence of polling. In addition, important feedback can and should be secured by means of dialogue with community influentials, municipal officials, labor group leaders, teacher group leaders, mass media personnel, and the like. There has been no intent to suggest that election strategy be based on poll results to the exclusion of feedback received from other sources.

We feel that ideally at least four opinion polls should be conducted in conjunction with a school election: (1) before deciding whether to hold the school election, (2) near the midpoint of intense campaign activity, (3) in the final days of the campaign, and (4) immediately following the election. Each of these polls should be carefully planned and executed. Each should sample enough people to insure that generalizations can be drawn from the group. The first poll will most often be designed to enable generalizations to be drawn for the total voter group and selected subgroups (e.g., the aged, the young, the lower class, the upper class, the business sector, the professional sector, the blue-collar sector). The same level of generalization is most often desired from the other polls, but polls during the campaign might also be designed to see what is happening within a particular "public." For example, the purpose may be to see what impact certain communication devices are having on the blue collar workers living in selected geographic areas of the district. If this is the case, the sample polled would be drawn from those subgroups. The postelection poll may be designed to find out why the voters residing in precincts with a heavy negative vote were opposed to the proposal under consideration. If so, the sample drawn should be representative of these precincts.

In hotly contested elections, more than two polls during the height of the campaign may be advisable. Some persons might question the

need for the postelection poll; however, because elections are frequent occurrences, the postelection poll can yield invaluable data for planning future campaigns. The authors fully recognize that conducting four or more polls is costly in time, money, and effort; but, if the results are used by school officials as a basis for campaign decision-making, the expenditures are justified.

Due to the number of variables in a given situation, no attempt has been made to offer estimates of the cost for taking a poll. The factors that have major effects on the direct cost of a given poll include: (a) whether the poll is conducted "in-house" or by an outside agency under contract, (b) the size and geographic spread of the sample, (c) the method of contact used, (d) the amount of information that must be secured from each respondent, and (e) the extent and method of data analysis. For example, a poll that includes 500 voters in the sample might have a direct cost of less than $500 if the poll is conducted in-house, the sample is chosen from the local telephone directory, contact is by telephone, only five closed-end questions are asked, and the data analysis consumes five minutes of on-line computer time. However, if the same size sample is chosen at random from throughout a large school district, the personal interview is the method of contact, and the poll is conducted by an outside agency, the direct cost might well increase tenfold, twenty-fold, or more. As a general rule, in-house polls incur the least direct cost. The next most economical are usually polls done by university groups holding the point of view that conducting such polls is a public service commitment and that educational benefits accrue from them to graduate students and staff. Polls conducted by private, professional polling groups are generally the most expensive. Well-conducted polls are relatively expensive; the timeworn axiom, "You get what you pay for," is generally applicable.

On the matter of sources of funds to pay for polls, two concepts are advanced. Polls conducted before a decision to call for an election might be financed from the "institutional research" budget of the district. The assumption is made that such an expenditure would probably not violate community norms, since at this point the poll is a source of feedback to enable the organization to respond to its environment. Polls conducted during an announced election campaign, however, should be paid for from private sources. The reasoning behind this assertion is that in many localities the legality of using public funds for such purposes is questionable, and often such an expenditure will violate community norms.

The point has been made that poorly conducted polls are worse than no polls. Accordingly, an effort has been made to define each step in the polling process. In review, the major steps are:

1. Define the purposes of the poll in enough detail to provide direction about the population to be sampled, the questions to be asked, and the data analysis to be done.

2. Select and organize the staff for the poll.

3. Develop a plan for the total effort, giving particular attention to time and tasks.

4. Decide on the method and size for the sampling procedure, and select the sample.

5. Select a method of contact.

6. Decide on the content, form of items, and format of the data-gathering instrument, and develop the instrument.

7. Try out the data-gathering instrument, revise it as needed, and reproduce it.

8. If interviewers are to be used, secure and train them.

9. Collect the data.

10. Prepare the data for analysis.

11. Analyze and synthesize the data consistent with the defined purposes.

12. Prepare a written report of the poll results and a series of suggestions for campaign strategy based on the results.

Many of these steps are interrelated and can occur concurrently.

Three major choices are made in the polling process: method of sample selection, sample size, and method of contact. There is a great temptation to take the least complicated route — a cluster sample, sample size arbitrarily based on a percentage of the population, and a mailed questionnaire. The authors believe that in most polling efforts the use of a probability sample (e.g., random, stratified random, or systematic), the determination of sample size based on the error that can be tolerated, and use of the personal interview method of contact will result in a better poll. We hold the personal conviction that unless there is a willingness to expend the necessary resources to insure, in so far as possible, that the poll will result in valid data from a representative sample of the "public" about which the educators want to generalize, they would be wise to forget polling and rely on feedback from other sources in developing election strategies.

The authors do not intend to imply that familiarity with the material presented here will make expert pollsters of school officials. If a

school district does not have staff members who possess the technical knowledge and depth of experience necessary to actually conduct a poll, the use of well-trained consultants is strongly advised. There may be situations in which the school leadership feels that the most feasible approach to opinion polling is to contract with an outside agency for the total effort. If such a contractual arrangement is to be used, the information presented in this chapter should be used in evaluating the capability of an outside agency to conduct an opinion poll, in defining the specifics of the contract, and in evaluating the quality of the work performed.

Suggested Readings

Cook, Desmond L. *Program Evaluation and Review Technique: Applications in Education*. Washington: U.S. Department of Health, Education, and Welfare, Office of Education, Bureau of Research, Cooperative Research Monograph No. 17, 1966.

Glock, Charles Y. (ed.). *Survey Research in the Social Sciences*. New York: Russell Sage Foundation, 1967.

Hauskin, Chester A. "Estimating Sample Size," *Journal of Research Services*, vol. 3, no. 1 (December 1963), pp. 3–4.

Moser, C. A. *Survey Methods in Social Investigation*, Chapters 10–15. London: Heinemann Educational Books, 1958.

Parten, Mildred. *Surveys, Polls, and Samples: Practical Procedures*, Chapters 2–17. New York: Harper and Brothers, 1950.

Rosenberg, Morris. *The Logic of Survey Analysis*. New York: Basic Books, 1968.

Sax, Gilbert. *Empirical Foundations of Educational Research*, Chapters 6, 9–10, 13. Englewood Cliffs, N.J.: Prentice-Hall, 1968.

Slonim, Morris J. "Sampling in a Nutshell," *Journal of American Statistical Association*, vol. 51, no. 278 (June 1957), pp. 143–61.

Stephan, Frederick F. and Phillip J. McCarthy. *Sampling Opinions: An Analysis of Survey Procedures*, Chapters 2–4, 8–9. New York: John Wiley and Sons, 1958.

Footnotes

1. Robert F. Mager, *Preparing Instructional Objectives* (Palo Alto, Cal.: Fearon Publishers, 1962).

2. Frederick F. Stephan and Phillip J. McCarthy, *Sampling Opinions: An Analysis of Survey Procedures* (New York: John Wiley and Sons, 1958), pp. 336–42.

3. Allen L. Edwards, *Statistical Methods for the Behavioral Sciences* (New York: Rinehart and Company, 1958), pp. 472–76.

4. W. Allen Wallis and Harry V. Roberts, *Statistics: A New Approach* (Glencoe, Ill.: The Free Press, 1956), pp. 631–35.

5. B. Seebohn Rowntree, *Poverty and Progress: A Second Social Survey of York* (London: Longmans, Green and Company, 1941), p. 489.

6. Chester A. Hauskin, "Estimating Sample Size," *Journal of Research Services*, vol. 3, no. 1 (December 1963), p. 3.

7. Gilbert Sax, *Empirical Foundations of Educational Research* (Englewood Cliffs, N.J.: Prentice-Hall, 1968), pp. 241–87.

8. Desmond L. Cook, *Program Evaluation and Review Technique: Applications in Education* (Washington: U.S. Department of Health, Education, and Welfare, Office of Education, Bureau of Research, Cooperative Research Monograph No. 17, 1966).

9. For an excellent description of such techniques, see Sidney Siegel, *Nonparametric Statistics for the Behavioral Sciences* (New York: McGraw-Hill Book Company, 1956).

5

Practical Considerations in Conducting School Election Campaigns

Much of the material presented thus far has been somewhat abstract and technical. A rationale for the participation of school leaders in school elections has been advanced and defended. Concepts, developed primarily from basic research, about political systems and voter behavior have been presented to provide an understanding of the milieu within which school elections occur. Drawing primarily from survey research methodology, considerable attention has been given to opinion polling procedures, on the assumption that polling is essential in planning for school elections and an area with which schoolmen have only limited familiarity. However, in the final analysis, winning school elections is more an art than a science. Therefore, this chapter focuses on very practical suggestions that experience has shown are useful in winning school elections.

Several perceptive school administrators have written accounts of their experiences in school elections. School elections have also been the subject of survey research material incorporated in doctoral dissertations. An illustrative bibliography of these materials is given in the suggested readings at the end of the chapter, and they are the basis of the suggestions presented in this chapter.

Even though the suggestions advanced have proved successful in given school districts at given times, indiscriminate use of these suggestions is not advocated. A careful examination of the environment of the school district should dictate the extent of their use.

The following discussion deals with (1) activity that should precede a decision to hold a school election, (2) organizing the campaign, (3) the role of professional staff and pupils, (4) communication techniques, (5) campaign literature, (6) dealing with the opposition, (7) getting the vote out, and (8) postelection activity.

Activities Before Deciding on an Election

Before making a decision to request an increase in the school district's operating levy, ask for a bond referendum for capital outlay, or call a referendum on some organizational matter, there are several steps school leaders should consider.

Develop the Proposal Carefully

In many school elections, voters are asked to ratify a proposal offered by the board of education as a solution to a pressing problem. That is, they are asked to approve a bond issue for new construction to relieve overcrowded conditions or replace obsolete facilities; they are asked to approve an increase in the millage levy to "buy" more educational services; or they are asked to approve a proposal for school district unification, as a means of improving the educational program. Such a school election proposal is presumably an outgrowth of recommendations from some data base (e.g., a comprehensive school survey, a building survey, a curriculum study, or a management study). If at all possible, outside consultants and influential lay citizens (see Chapter 2), as well as district personnel, should be involved in this proposal development activity.

Some studies indicate that the involvement of outside consultants and lay citizens is associated with success in elections.[1] For example, if the school officials feel there is a need for additional facilities in the school district, they might secure the services of an outside agency to conduct a building survey, with the stipulation that lay citizens be involved in the survey. This is not to suggest that lay citizens should collect or analyze the data on existing buildings and pupil population but that they could visit buildings, review the data, and assist in the projection of recommendations.

Based on his personal experience and survey data, Crosby, among others, has pointed out that citizen participation is among the most effective means of increasing citizen understanding.[2] The point is well illustrated by a successful bond election campaign in San Diego.[3] As a first step, the board of education appointed a citizens' review committee consisting of 152 representatives of the district's school neighborhoods and 21 business and civic leaders. The group met three times to review the data regarding current and future housing problems of the district. The result was that they strongly endorsed the superintendent's bond referendum proposal.

Throughout the review process, the proposal under consideration and the school leaders' position should be brutally examined for soundness. Schoolmen should recognize that their district is just one of many public agencies with justifiable needs seeking increased tax support, and that the taxpayer is constantly faced with the pressure of higher taxes. Therefore, school leaders are advised to ask themselves: "Can the proposal be justified in terms of teaching and learning? Are there other and perhaps cheaper proposals for achieving the same goals? Is this the wisest course of action for this school district at this time?"

Study Previous School Election Results

Grieder[4] and Mayer,[5] citing experiences within local districts, have stressed the importance of a postmortem on previous school elections, particularly if the district-sponsored proposal failed. If postelection poll results are available, a detailed review of them is in order. If not, a detailed analysis of the previous vote should be done. This will indicate potential sectors of strength and weakness (in terms of voting precincts and voter characteristics). An effort should also be made to discuss the previous elections in detail with informed local persons.

If the previous election resulted in failure, the discussions might be guided by such questions as:

1. Was the proposal hastily developed shortly before the election? The voters may have perceived the proposal as poorly developed and the election as held on too short a notice.

2. If school facilities were the issue, did the people view them as essential? If the voters disagreed with the proposed locations, did not see the need for new facilities, or felt planned facilities were "low priority," these views could have contributed to the defeat.

3. If an increase in the millage levy was the issue, was it viewed as excessive? The timing of an election, the demands of other public agencies, and the benefits to be derived, may have caused voters to consider that the tax increase was just "too much."

4. Who opposed the proposal? The evidence cited in Chapter 3 on voter behavior suggests that the personal factor is important in determining how people vote. The opposition of key opinion leaders may have been a major factor in the defeat. If there was organized opposition, educators must also ask whether there is any evidence that the opposition has diminished.

5. Did the voters really know what the proposal was all about? Some persons feel that voters often reject a proposal simply because they do not understand it. Thus, the defeat may have been a function of failure to communicate with the voters.

Assess the Opinions of the Leadership

In Chapter 2, a case was made for knowing the position of community influentials. Surveys have shown that the advice, approval, and active involvement of such persons is associated with success in elections.[6] Other surveys have shown that the support, or at least lack of opposition, of school board members,[7] municipal officials,[8] and citizen-teacher groups[9] exerts a positive influence on election outcomes. In this day of increasing "teacher voice" in school district policy matters, there is an obvious need to have teachers support a proposal, and their support cannot be taken for granted. One superintendent known to the authors carefully assesses teacher reaction before submitting a proposal to the electorate. He then makes an effort to insure that each teacher is registered to vote. In another local district with which the authors are familiar, the failure of a bond referendum was widely attributed to lack of support among the teachers.

Conduct a Districtwide Opinion Poll

Limited use has been made of results of well-conducted opinion polls as one basis for reaching decisions about school elections. One writer[10] with extensive experience in the field has stressed the importance of such polls. In at least two school districts, results of polls were reported to be helpful,[11] while in another district an election defeat was attributed in part to the failure to sample public opinion.[12] Use of such polls in national political campaigns has been well publicized.

The authors advocate the use of a "predecision poll," as discussed in Chapter 4. Such a poll should be designed to determine the voters' overall opinions about the schools, their concept of the needs of the school district, their sources of information about schools, and the like. These data will also be of benefit in identifying sectors of strength and weakness and communication techniques that might be used if the election is undertaken.

Examine the Following of the School Leaders

Both Barbour[13] and McDaniel[14] concluded, as a result of surveys, that respect for and confidence in the board of education and superintendent were almost always present in successful school bond referenda. Using his own experience and those of 50 superintendents, Crosby noted that a voter's personal feelings about teachers ranked high in helping him decide how to cast his vote.[15] Other evidence about the personal nature of the voting act was cited in Chapter 3.

The results of these experiences lead to the tentative conclusion that numerous school elections have been lost because of voters' personal opposition to a particular person or faction among the school leadership (both lay and professional) rather than because of opposition to the proposal under consideration. This was also discussed in Chapter 3. While recognizing the difficulty school officials have in "looking at themselves" and their close associates, each person in the school leadership should be carefully evaluated in terms of whether he is perceived favorably and has the confidence of the public or whether he represents a focus for controversy.

Select the Election Date Carefully

The results of the research activities discussed above will undoubtedly reveal some positive and some negative indications. If the decision is made to proceed with the election, and the choice of a date is open, school leaders should give careful thought to the time of the year when the election should be held. The relationship between the month of the year selected and the election outcome has been considered in several surveys.[16] Their findings suggest that (a) there is no "best" month (although October is more frequently associated with success), and (b) taxpaying months (particularly April), holiday seasons (December), and summer months (when school is not in session) are frequently associated with failure.

The election date selected can also be a factor in voter turnout. The percentage of registered voters voting is usually higher when the school election is held in conjunction with general state and national elections. Using common sense, educators may suppose that the greater the voter turnout the better the chances of success in school elections because of the "halo" assumed to be associated with education. Therefore, they will time the election to get a large turnout of

voters. If a low percentage of voters turn out, a small, determined minority concentrating on such opposition slogans as "tax squeeze," "overpaid school administrators," "waste of the tax dollar," and "educational palaces" can control the election outcome more easily. However, survey findings on the relationship between the percentage of voters casting votes and the election outcome are at best inconclusive. Surveys have shown that a "positive" outcome is associated with a high percentage turnout,[17] a low percentage turnout,[18] and a normal turnout.[19] Thus the "yes" vote may be more important than the massive vote.

Insure that Legal Requirements are Met

Many states have specific statutes governing notice of school elections; others do not. These statutes generally specify the length of time before an election that notification must be given and the means of notification to be used. In the absence of specific statutes, the school leadership must make a reasonable effort to publicize the election throughout the school district. If there are statutes, they should be carefully followed. The authors are aware of one school district in which a bond issue failed to be validated because of a legal technicality, even though the vote was overwhelmingly in favor of it. Garber, in reviewing a Missouri case, noted that courts are reluctant to set aside a school election for failure to follow the statutes "to the letter" unless there is clear evidence that the failure interfered with the election outcome.[20] However, he emphasized that school officials should "lean over backward" in following the law and being fair. The point is that battles over technicalities should be avoided, even though legally the school leaders might win, because the litigation will be expensive, relationships with the public will suffer, and school improvements will be delayed.

Campaign Organizations

The annals of experience are replete with attempts to run school election campaigns without careful organization. This is ridiculous. School children are valuable enough to merit that effective organization be mounted in their behalf. Those in control of school elections *must organize!* In hotly contested elections the side that has the best organization will win. This is true of all forms of political activity.

Obviously, there is no single blueprint for organizing. The organizational arrangement that has proved successful in one school district cannot be transferred intact to another school district and be expected to work in the same manner. However, surveys and testimonials based on experience emphasize that whatever organizational arrangement is developed, it must insure that (a) there is overall coordination of the campaign; (b) there is wide, visible, and well-organized lay citizen participation in the campaign; (c) information about the election and the proposal reaches each household; (d) effective and informed speakers are available for civic clubs, service clubs, and the like; (e) campaign literature is carefully developed and widely distributed; (f) personal contact is made with most if not all voters; (g) most or all potential "yes" voters are identified, registered (if necessary), and encouraged to vote on election day; (h) funds are raised to finance the campaign adequately; (i) public endorsements are secured from influential persons and groups; (j) functional contact is made with the mass media; (k) there is contact with special interest groups — taxpayer groups, service clubs, realtors, unions, civic clubs, other taxing bodies, and the like; (l) campaign workers are secured and oriented; (m) information is provided to campaign workers to enable them to answer questions most often raised by voters; and (n) campaign workers are regularly provided with information on the progress of the campaign. The discussion that follows illustrates many of these facets of organization. Later in this chapter special attention is given to the role of the professional staff and pupils, communication techniques, campaign literature, and getting the vote out.

William W. Allen, a man with over 20 years of experience in public relations work, who has long been active in citizen involvement in public school affairs, has suggested that the campaign be basically organized around a citizens' committee.[21] He suggests that if a six- to eight-week intensive campaign is planned, the first half of the period should be devoted exclusively to organizing, recruiting, and planning. According to Allen, the campaign could be headed by a general chairman who is not an educator or a member of the board of education. The citizens could be organized into four major groups (each headed by a chairman) — a publicity and promotion committee, contact with special groups committee, finance committee, and get-out-the-vote committee. The publicity and promotion group should handle public information and advertisement through the mass media, pamphlets, brochures, local business and industry publi-

cations, and the like. The contact with special groups committee should establish and maintain contact with community groups identified as being influential in the election. The finance committee should be charged with raising the funds needed to run the campaign. The get-out-the-vote committee is seen by Allen as the real key to success. He suggests dividing the district into geographic sectors (e.g., ten square blocks in the city or an area encompassing 50—70 voters in the open country), appointing a captain for each sector, and securing a leader for each city block or 15 rural voters. These leaders comprise the get-out-the-vote committee. Following a thorough orientation, they are assigned the task of personal contacts with each voter.

The succesful San Diego election referred to previously provides a good illustration of wide and well-organized community involvement.[22] The campaign was under the direction of a 15-member executive committee. Its members were chosen from among the opinion leaders and from school-based committees that were organized for the campaign. (Virtually every testimonial stresses the importance of having citizen groups include opinion leaders in the community, representatives of the several segments of the voting population, and representatives of each political party.) Within each of the 152 school communities, a committee of citizens was organized under the guidance of a chairman. Each of the school-based committees set its own financial goals, means of raising money, and methods of voter contact. Communication among the school-based groups was facilitated by a newsletter to each person on each committee. A speakers' bureau was formed and public endorsements were secured from over 100 organized groups and approximately 20 prominent persons in the community. In total, the campaign involved over 5,000 volunteer workers.

Hall's report of a school bond campaign in Evanston, Illinois, well illustrates the need for careful coordination among the several groups working in the campaign.[23] In Evanston the elementary school district board and high school district board, both faced with facility needs, joined forces in a campaign that began some 15 months before election day. A committee composed of educators was formed to provide general direction, to work through teachers and pupils, and to arrange conferences with municipal bodies, women voter groups, political party groups, civic groups, and the like. The high school PTA and Lay Advisory Council conducted a series of block meetings

at which local teacher organization personnel distributed information and made presentations. The elementary PTA groups followed with a second series of "block coffees." A citizens' committee composed of 49 prominent persons was organized to recruit volunteer workers. Through this group a work headquarters was established, funds were supplied for campaign literature, and the literature was distributed. In the final week of the campaign a door-to-door canvass was conducted by experienced political party precinct workers from both parties. On election day, teachers formed a transportation committee, and volunteer teachers and lay citizens served as "checkers" at the polls.

In a suburban Wilmington, Delaware, district, an organizational pattern similar to that suggested by Allen was used with success.[24] The pattern is shown in Figure 1.

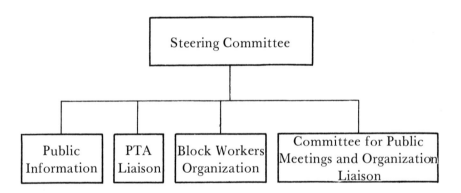

Figure 1. Organization Pattern in Wilmington, Delaware

Two men with a background in public relations served as cochairmen of the public information group, which developed campaign materials translating school information into a language that could be easily and quickly understood by the public. The PTA group paid for brochure printing and organized a telephone campaign. The block worker group had the assignment of getting the district's message into each household. To do this, the district was divided into 20 geographic areas. Within each area a chairman was appointed, a captain was chosen for each of the housing developments, and block workers were selected for each 10 households. To insure information accuracy, an educator was assigned to each captain as a resource

person and researcher. Speaking engagements were handled by citizens from the public meetings group.

In many campaigns, the arrangements for providing informed speakers for group meetings and giving volunteer lay campaign workers the information they need to answer voters' questions are haphazard. The problems encountered with speakers are: (a) the lay citizen (and often the educator) may not be sufficiently knowledgeable to deal with complex problems and questions, (b) the educator is subject to the charge of "distorting the facts" or propagandizing, and (c) the designated speaker may not be able to fulfill the engagement. One solution might be to organize two-man speaker teams composed of a lay citizen and an informed educator, with the educator serving in a supportive role.

Birmingham, Michigan, successfully used three-man teams consisting of a lay citizen, an educator, and a school board member.[25] The lay citizen presented the budget proposals, the educator discussed personnel and curriculum needs, and the board member handled the question and answer session.

In an Alice, Texas, Independent School District campaign that was successful, two-man school administrator teams were formed, with the school superintendent excluded, and no speaker appeared before an organization to which he himself belonged.[26] Before any presentation was made to the public, it was made before the board of education. In each presentation, extensive use was made of audiovisual material. Since each team member was assigned to either the first or the second half of a presentation, if a member of the team could not be present, it was easy to find a replacement.

On the matter of providing lay campaign workers with the information they need to answer questions, the technique of the suburban Wilmington district in assigning an informed educator to each "working unit" has merit.[27] Also, many districts have found it helpful to provide each campaign worker with a fairly detailed question and answer manual covering frequently asked questions. In some instances appropriate responses to "hostile" questions frequently raised by the opposition have been included. In the Birmingham, Michigan, campaign referred to previously, each block worker received a 40-page manual with detailed information on the district's educational program, teaching staff, administration, facilities, and finances.[28]

Role of the Professional Staff and Pupils

Although the preceding section emphasized wide, visible, and well-organized citizen participation in school election campaigns, there is no intent to suggest that school personnel have a limited role with little responsibility. Educators must assume a strong and active supporting role. The testimonials and survey data presented earlier in this chapter show that school leaders should (a) assume leadership in developing the proposal with the aid of opinion leaders, municipal officials, teacher organization personnel, and the like; (b) assess opinions and the "following" of key persons; (c) insure that the needed "research" is conducted (e.g., analysis of previous elections and opinion sampling); (d) insure that the legal requirements for elections are met; (e) plan and organize the citizen effort; (f) serve as resource persons; (g) insure that the citizen workers are oriented and have the "hard data" they need; and (h) aid communication among the several groups involved in the campaign.

In several of the illustrations of successful campaigns cited, the educators were "visible" as speakers before various community groups; in some instances they assumed no such responsibilities. There is some tenuous survey data to suggest that voters like to get information directly from school leaders.[29] To suggest that school personnel should or should not be used as speakers before community groups would be fallacious. However, if school personnel are used as speakers, they should take care to stick to the facts and not appear to be making a "hard sell."

The material in the previous sections has already implied some responsibilities for school officials in relation to the mass media. The findings from a study in suburban Chicago indicated that there were some correlations between number of votes cast and election outcome and certain facets of newspaper coverage (e.g., article length, location, bias, and editorial position).[30] In many urban areas, every utterance and action of school leaders is subject to coverage and analysis by the press, radio, and television. Therefore, the writers strongly urge that school officials begin early and continue throughout the campaign to communicate with persons such as local newspaper publishers and editors, and owners and directors of local radio and television stations. They will often be among the local opinion leaders. Obviously, the school officials will be seeking favorable editorials, extensive coverage, and newspaper articles well placed in specific issues. If the assumption is valid that the opposition of local

mass media can be very damaging to the school district's proposal, school leaders might well try to get the media to take a neutral position if support is not forthcoming. They could urge media leaders to be silent editorially and objective in reporting, at the very least.

Often school pupils are used in campaigns, most frequently as couriers to get material into the homes. In a winning Des Moines, Iowa, campaign, some 43,500 pupils took home a four-page paper explaining the proposal and background situation.[31] Just before electon day over 26,000 elementary pupils went home with "VOTE" tags. Pupils have been known to organize pickets and public demonstrations in support of a school district's proposal. In one situation observed by the authors, pupils organized and conducted a march on city hall in support of the school leaders' position. However, many voters viewed the pupils' activity as having the tacit approval of the school officials and resented such tactics. The result was a defeat for the school proposal.

Because indiscriminate use of pupils may be viewed as exploitation of children, caution should be observed in involving pupils. For example, sending pupils home with notices of the election, election dates, notices of public meetings, and facts that have appeared in the local press may be acceptable, but to use the children to distribute campaign "propaganda" may not.

Communication Techniques

There is some evidence (see Chapter 3) that many people make up their minds early in a campaign and that information received during a campaign does not often change their votes. However, other voters are "cross-pressured," and likely to decide on the issue late in the campaign. There is some evidence that the extent of communication and the degree to which people are informed of school needs are crucial factors in an election outcome.[32] Therefore, throughout the campaign considerable emphasis should be placed on communication with the voters.

Since people get information from a variety of sources, a wide variety of communication techniques should be employed. Support for such a generalization was found in the results of a postelection questionnaire poll conducted by one local district.[33] The poll indicated that (a) almost 98 percent of the respondents read the mailed

literature, (b) public meetings devoted to the issue influenced over 33 percent in a positive manner, (c) newspaper and television reports influenced 28 percent, and (d) 24 percent were influenced by word of mouth.

In the previously mentioned San Diego campaign, the techniques used included speakers to a variety of groups, home leaflets, automobile bumper stickers, well-placed billboard ads, cards on and in public buses, newspaper ads, television and radio spot announcements, window cards for retail outlets, person-to-person contact, and the placement of an ad on milk bottle tops by a local dairy.[34] In Des Moines, speakers for churches, civic clubs, and service groups were used; some 35,000 six-page leaflets were distributed; 12 billboard ads were used; approximately 31,500 post cards were mailed just before election day to persons who had signed the petition requesting the election; some 43,500 four-page papers were sent into homes by students; just before election day the elementary students went home with "VOTE" tags; and in the last ten days, 300 volunteer workers contacted the homes in precincts where there had been a 50 percent or better "yes" vote in the previous school bond election.[35]

These two illustrations suggest that a variety of communication techniques are available in a school election campaign. The creativity of campaign leaders should be encouraged in developing useful techniques. For example, one effective method used in an Evanston, Illinois, campaign was a ten-minute motion picture, produced by teachers and pupils, entitled, "A Crowded Day at Evanston High."[36]

Based on his experience and survey research, Crosby stressed the importance of neighbors and newspapers in helping voters decide. [37] A Cuyahoga Falls, Ohio, opinion poll showed that newspapers were the best means of getting information to voters.[38] Therefore, the authors reemphasize the need for organizing citizen "block workers" to visit the homes and for working with the local press in an effort to secure editorial support and extensive coverage.

Format and Content of Campaign Literature

Attention must be given to the appearance and substance of the literature used in campaigns. In the paragraphs that follow, suggestions in this regard are offered.

Simplicity Is Important

Allen suggests that the three or four main arguments for the district's proposal should be carefully identified. Then he advises: "Confine the campaign to these three or four main points. Most voters don't want to know as much as the administrator or school board, and couldn't remember it all if they wanted to hear it. The simple, honest, direct approach is always best."[3 9]

Crosby, drawing on extensive experience and survey data, probably stated the point best when he said:

Too much school bond literature is about as readable and inviting as a weather bureau report. Graphs, charts, tables — these hold little interest for the bridge devotee, the factory worker, the housewife, or many professional people. Keep the language simple and to the point. Pitch it to the man on the street. Never use the word "needs"; use "opportunities" instead, and remember that the public has little idea of what the term "mill" means. It is best not used.[40]

The voices of experience are clear — concentrate your material on a few key points, avoid minute details, make it attractive and readable, and avoid educational jargon.

The simplicity of material is also related to how expensive it looks. Carter and DeVries, among others, expressed the opinion that very ornate and expensive-looking materials may have an adverse affect on voters.[4 1] Regardless of the cost, one means of allaying any feeling that public money is being used in the production of campaign literature is to stress the use of private funds. For example, each piece of campaign literature can note in a conspicuous place: "This pamphlet was prepared and paid for by The Citizens' Committee for Better Schools, P.O. Box 1234, Zach Township."

Emphasize Objectives

The objectives that can be accomplished by successful passage of the proposal should be stressed. Show what "payoff" passage of the proposal has for the community and its people. To be a bit crass, show what is in it for each sector of the community, if possible. For example, if it is a proposal for capital outlay bonds, stress how the location of new schools and improvements to existing schools will better serve children. The "what's in it" is extremely important for childless couples, the unmarried, and senior citizens who derive no

direct benefit from schools in terms of children to be educated. The appeal to such persons might stress how better educational opportunities make better communities, thus increasing property values and attracting more persons to share the tax load. (Two west coast districts used an interesting technique to hold the interest of senior citizens: They formed "Gold Card Clubs" — each citizen, 60 years old or over, was issued a card that entitled him to admission to senior high school student-body-sponsored public events, such as plays, concerts, and athletic events.)[42]

Focus on the Children

A report of two bond campaigns in Crystal Lake, Illinois — the first a failure and the second a success — compared key brochures for each campaign.[43] The brochure used in the first and unsuccessful campaign shows a picture of the proposed new high school building, and a caption giving its name, location, and capacity. The brochure of the second and successful campaign shows 11 attractive children with schoolbooks, and a caption reading, "Our Children and Our High School Needs." The experience in this school district illustrates the point — make the materials child-centered. Stress services to children and not cost to the taxpayers. For example, schoolmen can use pictures of individual children with themes such as "Support Proposition 1 so Jimmy can have a desk of his own," "11,742 children are now on half-day sessions," "5,400 children are now in substandard classrooms," "14,000 more children are expected in our schools by 1975," or "Your child needs your help now."

Other writers have made this point in a slightly different manner. They stress the need for emotional appeal in the campaign literature. The details of the situation — the cold facts — are essential in telling the story; however, people often make a decision about an issue based in large measure upon the emotional impact it has on them. Campaign material should be attractive from this point of view. To illustrate, all material might carry the picture of a single child with the slogan: "Your Responsibility — His Future," or the picture of a group of children and "If These Kids Don't Make It, Neither Do We." Emotion-laden slogans have long been a fact of political life in the United States — because they're effective.

Dealing with the Cost

Crosby advises that, in presenting the cost of a proposal, school-men should have one spot in a brochure for "Hard, Cold Facts," where the cost is indicated in a factual manner without "covering up" in any way.[44] Then don't mention cost again. The message is to play up educational services to children and play down educational cost. One school administrator put it this way: "Throughout the bond drive we talked buildings and dollars. When we stopped to listen to our voters, we heard them talking children and learning. That's what we should have been saying all along."[45]

In citing cost figures, the concept of simplicity is again important. More specifically, in dealing with the cost of the proposal, reduce it to the cost per individual family. To the man-on-the-street, the total cost of a proposal may appear staggering. Also, he wants to know what it is going to cost him personally. Therefore, rather than focusing on comprehensive figures, costs should be broken down. For example, if a bond issue is to be paid for by real estate taxes, the theme might be: "If your last year's taxes were $300, your *yearly* cost for these school bonds (principal and interest) will be $16; your total *weekly* cost for our children will be 31¢." One district's brochure showed three homes of differing value, and at a glance a taxpayer could determine his approximate cost per year and per month. Furthermore, the yearly cost was equated to such items as a woman's housedress, two steak dinners, or a pair of men's shoes.[46]

Positive Approaches

"If the millage levy is not increased, we'll be forced to curtail services. My recommendation to the board is that we start with interscholastic athletics." This threat by an unnamed superintendent acquaintance, which he probably could not have carried out, might have seemed to frighten the voters into supporting his budget proposal; however, the long range impact in terms of community support is obviously damning. The testimonials of successful experience and surveys of school election campaigns show, either explicitly or implicitly, that campaign material should be positive in content. Objectives, benefits to be derived, and educational services should be accented in an honest, straightforward manner. Avoid threat, high pressure, shame, and appeal to prejudice in campaign literature.

Highlight Support

In previous sections of this chapter the need for support from the board of education and various other individuals and groups in the community was demonstrated. Our last suggestion about the substance of campaign material is simple — show this support in the campaign literature. For example, "These groups have endorsed Proposal A: Zach Township PTA, the Zach Chamber of Commerce, Office and Professional Employees Local 1234," or "Jim Bolles says he is voting "Yes" on Proposal A."

The importance of publicizing support from the various sectors of the community cannot be overemphasized. One superintendent publicly acknowledged that the "yes" vote in his district was increased because of a supporting editorial statement in the local Catholic newspaper by the bishop of the diocese.[4][7]

Dealing with the Opposition

In any election campaign school officials should expect strong opposition. They should also expect the "worst" from the opposition in terms of campaign tactics. That is, the opposition might publicize half-truths, make charges that cannot be supported by the data, distort the meaning of the data, engage in personal attacks, appeal to group prejudice, and insert irrelevant issues into the campaign as a smokescreen. For example, Thompson reported that in the previously described San Diego campaign the opposition made an effort to relate the district's de facto segregation problems to the bond issue.[4][8]

Often the most immediate tendency of school administrators is to respond to each charge. Such action is ill advised — more than one school election has been lost by playing according to the opposition's rules. To use the jargon of today's youth, the school official should "keep his cool" and "follow his game plan." In the San Diego situation this was what occurred; the school leaders refused to get sidetracked, insisting that two separate issues were at stake. This is not to say that it is inappropriate to correct the record and prepare campaign workers with answers that can be supported by the data, for the more frequent questions raised by the opposition.

At a more specific level, the following suggestions are offered:

1. When dealing with a person who does not agree with the logic being advanced, the school supporter should not argue. He can state

his position positively and calmly, and support it by focusing on the objectives to be achieved for children. If the antagonist persists, the best course of action for the school advocate is to reply in a courteous vein that he is sorry his position is not understood and accepted, but he respects the right of the other to disagree.

2. It is best not to engage in extemporaneous public debate. Often in a give and take public forum following a presentation in support of the proposal, some person in the audience with an opposing view will raise an irrelevant and perhaps unanswerable question. The wise procedure is to repeat the positions necessary to support the proposal and not to attempt to engage in a debate based on such a question, because it gives the opposition a platform and the attempted response may be viewed as evasive.

3. Do not persist with those who have made up their mind. Once it is obvious that a person and/or group is firm in their position, recognize it and "retire gracefully."

4. A favorable press is not assured. If the press is unfavorable, editorials will reflect this, and the news reported may be unfairly slanted. In such a situation, educators should not respond by "letters to the editor" and attacks on the press during personal appearances, in campaign literature, and in presentations through other mass media. Rather they should stay with their campaign strategy, remembering that the press is in a favored position in such an encounter. An attempt may be made to secure support or neutralize the press by means of private and reasoned dialogue with the publisher or editor.

5. Never personally attack or ridicule the opponents or their reasoning. Often the group in support of the school district's proposal is composed of the more highly educated and civic-minded persons in the community; as such, they may view some members of the opposition and their positions as uninformed, reactionary, and illogical. To belittle the opponents, however, does nothing more than provide them with free publicity and may incur the antagonism of undecided voters. Do not make the opposition "martyrs with cause."

In the testimonials of schoolmen on successful experiences, the advice most frequently offered is, in effect, that educators must carefully develop their strategy and stay with it. This is the essence of the message offered here, and it is particularly sound advice if opinion poll results show that the school district's proposal has majority support. However, if poll results show that certain of the opposition's charges have gained considerable credence, and the pro-

posal therefore does not have majority support, chances must be taken and an effort made to respond to the charges. In such cases, the suggestions made above about campaign material will be useful.

Getting Out the Vote

In view of the inconclusive nature of evidence on the relationship between the percentage of voters voting and success in school elections, high priority should be placed on getting the potential "yes" voters to the polls on election day. After four straight bond issue defeats, forgetting about the "no" voters and worrying about the nonvoters was the basic formula applied in Mill Valley, California. The result was victory.[49]

As with other aspects of a successful campaign, organization and planning are essential in getting out the "yes" voters. A review of the successful campaigns cited earlier in this chapter, suggests that the most feasible approach is probably through a block workers' organization composed of volunteer lay citizens. The block workers should be organized, be oriented, and begin their activity well in advance of the closing date for voter registration. As a first step, individual workers should visit every household in "their block" leaving information about the upcoming election (dates, the issue, polling places, voter registration procedures, and the like), answering questions, determining the names of adults within the household and their voter registration status, and assessing sentiment about the upcoming election. As a next step, the list of persons who think they are properly registered to vote should be checked against the updated registered voter list to insure that each is in fact registered. Next a list of unregistered (including any who felt they were registered but were not) and positively leaning or cross-pressured persons should be prepared and each one urged to register. The "please register" plea should be accompanied by an offer to assist with transportation, baby sitting services, and the like. Followup calls between the close of voter registration and election day should be made to answer questions, distribute additional campaign material, and further assess voter preference. (In this connection it is probably more fruitful to concentrate the block workers' energy on providing information to the undecided and on reassuring the "yes" voter than to spend countless hours on the hard-core opposition.) On the eve of election day each potential "yes" voter should be contacted and reminded of

the election (again with an offer to assist if needed in getting the voter to the polls). The contact process should be repeated late in the afternoon of election day; if the voter has not been to the polls, a last plea and offer of assistance should be made.

The evidence suggests that the group composed of married couples with school age or preschool age children usually contains the largest proportion of potential "yes" voters. This group may also contain a large percent of apathetic persons and cross-pressured persons. Therefore, every effort should be made within this group. However, concentrating on this group to the exclusion of groups that have been identified as potential "no" voters (e.g., large property owners, retired persons, apartment dwellers, parents of parochial school pupils, and the like) is not advised. An appropriate appeal might result in some support from within such groups. The appeal should be one of hope — not fear or shame.

Postelection Activity

School executives anxiously examine the vote totals following an election. If the outcome is positive, they are gratified and feel reinforced; if it is negative, they are understandably dejected. Either way, however, the authors fear that far too often schoolmen go ahead with the job of administering the district school program taking little definitive action related to the school election. This behavior can easily create the impression among the citizens that they are forgotten by school personnel except when their vote is coveted. The reader should remember that win or lose, in most districts, school elections are an ever-recurring phenomenon. Therefore, certain postelection steps should be taken by school leaders.

First, appropriate appreciation should be expressed to the people. This can be done through the mass media to the voters, but personal letters of appreciation should be sent to key individuals, campaign workers, and groups. If the campaign was successful, wide public recognition should be given to individuals and groups who were influential in the achievement.

Second, regardless of the outcome, a precinct by precinct analysis of the vote should be made. This will identify areas of strength and weakness, which is invaluable information for future school elections.

Third, a postelection opinion poll should be seriously considered.

As previously noted, conducting a poll is not an easy task, but the benefits may justify the effort. "It is as valuable as the priceless point after touchdown. You know how people voted, but what influenced their vote? How long before election did they decide? A good opinion poll will give you answers to use next time."[50]

Fourth, keep the people informed of the steps being taken within the school district as a result of the election outcome. For example, if the election was for school construction bonds, and was successful, inform the people as progress is made in the building program.

Suggested Readings

Allen, William W. "Steps to Successful Campaigns for School Bond Issues and Tax Referenda," *Illinois Education*, vol. 56, no. 6 (February 1968), pp. 257–59.

Bloome, Arvin C. "Can We Stem the Tide in Our School Bond Elections?" *American School Board Journal*, vol. 150, no. 3 (March 1965), pp. 62–63.

Carter, Boyd, and Ted DeVries. "Ten Commandments of Successful School Tax Campaigns," *Clearing House*, vol. 42, no. 4 (December 1967), pp. 210–12.

Crosby, Otis A. "How to Make Bonds a Winning Issue," *Nation's Schools*, vol. 72, no. 1 (July 1963), pp. 27–28.

–––. "How to Prepare Winning Bond Issues," *Nation's Schools*, vol. 81, no. 4 (April 1968), pp. 81–82.

Denny, Robert R., and John H. Harris. "Active Citizens' Committee Wins School Bond Election," *American School Board Journal*, vol. 149, no. 3 (September 1964), pp. 21–22.

Hall, J. Floyd. "How Evanston Passed Its Bond Issue," *NEA Journal*, vol. 54, no. 9 (December 1965), pp. 42–44.

"How One District Reversed a Bond Defeat," *School Management*, vol. 6, no. 3 (March 1962), pp. 93–95.

Mayer, Frank C. "How to Find Out Why the Voters Said No," *School Management*, vol. 11, no. 10 (October 1967), pp. 78–79.

Stabile, Robert. "Districts Win Bond Issues the Hard Way," *Nation's Schools*, vol. 79, no. 5 (May 1967), pp. 77–78.

Thompson, Dorothy. "An Informed Public 'Buys' Bonds," *American School Board Journal*, vol. 155, no. 1 (July 1967), pp. 18–22.

Westie, Charles M. "Voter Opinion Survey," *Michigan Education Journal*, vol. 43, no. 15 (March 1966), pp. 22–24, 40, 42.

Footnotes

1. Edwin L. Barbour, "Effects of Socio-Economic Factors on School Bond Elections in Iowa" (doctoral thesis, Iowa State University, 1966); Billy N. Crosswait, "Factors Related to the Success and Failure of Bond Issues in the Independent School Districts of South Dakota" (doctoral thesis, University of South Dakota, 1967); Donald F. Kenny, "A Functional Analysis of Citizens' Committees During School Financial Elections" (doctoral thesis, Stanford University, 1962).

2. Otis A. Crosby, "How to Prepare Winning Bond Issues," *Nation's Schools*, vol. 81, no. 4 (April 1968), pp. 81—82.

3. Dorothy Thompson, "An Informed Public 'Buys' Bonds," *American School Board Journal*, vol. 155, no. 1 (July 1967), pp. 18—22.

4. Calvin Grieder, "The Administrators Clinic," *Nation's Schools*, vol. 70, no. 2 (August 1962), pp. 6, 10.

5. Frank C. Mayer, "How to Find Out Why the Voters Said No," *School Management*, vol. 11, no. 10 (October 1967), pp. 78—79.

6. Joe W. Harper, "A Study of Community Power Structure in Certain School Districts in the State of Texas and Its Influence on Bond Elections" (doctoral thesis, North Texas State University, 1965); Charles P. McDaniel, Jr., "A Study of Factors Affecting the Outcome of School Bond Issues in Selected Georgia School Districts" (doctoral thesis, University of Georgia, 1967); Arvin C. Bloome, "Can We Stem the Tide in Our School Bond Elections?" *American School Board Journal*, vol. 150, no. 3 (March 1965), pp. 62—63.

7. Russell J. Crider, "Identification of Factors Which Influence the Passage or Failure of School Bond Issues in Selected Counties of Mississippi" (doctoral thesis, University of Southern Mississippi, 1967); McDaniel, *op. cit.*

8. Crider, *op. cit.*; Prentice L. Gott, "Selected Factors Associated with the Success or Failure of School Bond Issue Campaigns in Kentucky" (doctoral thesis, George Peabody College of Teachers, 1962).

9. Crider, *op. cit.*

10. William W. Allen, "Steps to Successful Campaigns for School Bond Issues and Tax Referenda," *Illinois Education*, vol. 56, no. 6 (February 1968), pp. 257—59.

11. Robert Stabile, "Districts Win Bond Issues the Hard Way," *Nation's Schools*, vol. 79, no. 5 (May 1967), pp. 77—78; Charles M. Westie, "Voter Opinion Survey," *Michigan Education Journal*, vol. 43, no. 15 (March 1966), pp. 22—24, 40, 42.

12. "How One District Reversed a Bond Defeat," *School Management*, vol. 6, no. 3 (March 1963), pp. 93—95.

13. Barbour, *op. cit.*

14. McDaniel, *op. cit.*

15. Otis A. Crosby, "How to Make Bonds a Winning Issue," *Nation's Schools*, vol. 72, no. 1 (July 1963), pp. 27—28.

16. Crider, *op. cit.*; Crosby, "How to Prepare Winning Bond Issues," *loc. cit.*; Holly W. Mitchell, Jr., "Identification and Evaluation of Factors Affecting School Bond Issues in Missouri Public Schools" (doctoral thesis, University of Missouri, 1962); Edward V. Murphy, "Selected Variables in the Success of Bond

Elections in California School Districts" (doctoral thesis, University of Southern California, 1966).

17. Crosswait, *op. cit.*

18. Sidney Dykstra, "A Study of the Relationships of Non-Public School Enrollment to the Approval of School Millage and Bond Proposals" (doctoral thesis, University of Michigan, 1964).

19. Murphy, *op. cit.*

20. Lee O. Garber, "School Bond Election Notice Should be Publicized Fully and Fairly, Displayed Conspicuously," *Nation's Schools*, vol. 69, no. 2 (February 1962), pp. 82, 104.

21. Allen, *loc. cit.*

22. Thompson, *loc. cit.*

23. J. Floyd Hall, "How Evanston Passed Its Bond Issue," *NEA Journal*, vol. 54, no. 9 (December 1965), pp. 42—44.

24. Leroy C. Olson, "Second Effort Turned a Losing Bond Issue Around," *Nation's Schools*, vol. 78, no. 3 (September 1966), pp. 62—64.

25. William Lyman and Walter S. Piel, "How Laymen Helped Put Over a Budget Vote," *School Management*, vol. 6, no. 10 (October 1962), pp. 95—98.

26. W. W. Farrar, "District Staff Sold Board and Public on New Financing," *Nation's Schools*, vol. 78, no. 3 (September 1966), pp. 62—63.

27. Olson, *loc. cit.*

28. Lyman and Piel, *loc. cit.*

29. Richard F. Carter, "Voters and Their Schools," *Phi Delta Kappan*, vol. 42, no. 6 (March 1961), pp. 241—49.

30. Ralph H. Lieber, "An Analysis and the Relationship of Weekly Community Suburban Papers to the Outcome of School Voting Issues" (doctoral thesis, Northwestern University, 1967).

31. Robert R. Denny and John H. Harris, "Active Citizens' Committee Wins School Bond Election," *American School Board Journal*, vol. 149, no. 3 (September 1964), pp. 21—22.

32. Gott, *op. cit.*; Mitchell, *op. cit.*

33. LaVerne H. Boss and Michael Thomas, "Bond Issue Survey: Mail Campaigns Pay Off," *Nation's Schools*, vol. 81, no. 4 (April 1968), p. 82.

34. Thompson, *loc. cit.*

35. Denny and Harris, *loc. cit.*

36. Hall, *loc. cit.*

37. Crosby, "How to Make Bonds a Winning Issue," *loc. cit.*

38. Stabile, *loc. cit.*

39. Allen, *op. cit.*, p. 258.

40. Crosby, "How to Make Bonds a Winning Issue," *op. cit.*, p. 28.

41. Boyd Carter and Ted DeVries, "Ten Commandments of Successful School Tax Campaigns," *Clearing House*, vol. 42, no. 4 (December 1967), pp. 210—12.

42. Jo Jenkins, "Senior Citizens: How to Perk Up Their Interest in Schools," *American School Board Journal*, vol. 156, no. 2 (August 1968), p. 15.

43. "How One District Reversed a Bond Defeat," *op. cit.*, pp. 94—95.

44. Crosby, "How to Make Bonds a Winning Issue," *op. cit.*, p. 28.

45. "How to Win a Lost Bond Vote," *School Management*, vol. 8, no. 11 (November 1964), p. 73.

46. Ernest M. Hanson, "Bond Issue Brochure Wins an Election and School-men's Applause," *Nation's Schools*, vol. 76, no. 1 (July 1965), p. 29.

47. Denny and Harris, *op. cit.*, p. 22.

48. Thompson, *loc. cit.*

49. "How to Bounce Back from a Bond Issue Defeat," *School Management*, vol. 7, no. 11 (November 1963), pp. 57–62.

50. Crosby, "How to Make Bonds a Winning Issue," *op. cit.*, p. 28.

6

Modern
Political Techniques

Much of the knowledge about educational administration before World War II was based upon practice in small school districts. Three decades ago there were more than 115,000 local school districts in the nation. Educational administration had a rural, agrarian orientation during the 1930's and early 1940's.

In 1970 there were fewer than 18,000 operating local school districts. The conditions in which school administrators practice and school boards serve have changed radically since the end of World War II. An urban, technologically oriented society exists. Population mobility is much greater than a person in the 1940's could have imagined. Recent social developments have changed the climate in which school elections must be conducted.

In the typical rural school district with a small population, there is greater likelihood of agreement concerning the kind of schools desired. There is less chance of high levels of controversy among citizens. There is greater possibility that the public will have confidence in the board of education and the school administrators because informal processes of interaction are possible. As a consequence, a proposal from the board that is subject to a referendum has less possibility of generating heated controversy.

The growth in size and complexity of large school districts may make controversy in school elections more likely there than in small school districts. The board members and school administrators of large city and consolidated school districts have fewer opportunities to know and communicate personally and directly with citizens. Many of them fail to compensate for this by communicating well with leaders in the school district power structure. As a consequence

of these conditions, there is greater chance of public loss of confidence in education leaders. This in itself creates a seedbed for high levels of controversy and defeat for school-board-sponsored proposals in school elections.

Crain, Katz, and Rosenthal, in a study discussed in Chapter 3, found that high levels of controversy usually reduced the chances of a vote in favor of fluoridating the city's water system.[1] There is reason to believe that the same condition would apply in educational elections. In the new politics of large school districts, education leaders must accept the fact that there will be conflict and confrontation. They must aim in their political leadership to reduce the level of conflict and controversy, but recognize that they will seldom eliminate it entirely. A low level of controversy about school board proposals may assist in their passage. Thus, the goal is to keep controversy from reaching a high pitch.

Given the potential for conflict and controversy and the lack of personal contact, due to the district's size and mobile population, school leaders need some understanding of the possibilities of "new politics" — particularly the use of television in election campaigns. Since extensive use of television greatly increases campaign costs, knowledge of modern funding techniques is also needed.

The first part of this chapter discusses techniques of the "new politics" concept. The material on which this discussion is based is drawn primarily from the writings of astute observers and researchers concerned with partisan election campaigns for national and statewide public offices. In an effort to provide some synthesis, the second part of the chapter deals with the implications of modern political techniques for school elections.

The New Politics

Much has been written in recent years about the so-called new politics. The new politics were discussed as early as the 1952 presidential election. In that campaign the word "image" first came into widespread use in politics. A major feature in the closing weeks of the Eisenhower campaign was a series of "spot" commercials — "Eisenhower Answers America" — prepared by an advertising firm.[2] The new politics became a much discussed topic following John F. Kennedy's election in 1960. Theodore H. White succeeded in popularizing the campaigns of the different candidates in that presidential election in his Pulitzer Prize winning book.[3]

What is new about the new politics? An off-the-cuff answer is that it is campaigning via television. However, this is an inadequate response. Certainly television is the big new ingredient in the new politics. Packaging material for the media and creating an image to be projected via television are two of the main techniques. However, more is involved in the new politics than the selling (or marketing) of candidates by television. The new politics require the expenditure of huge sums of money. Direct use of experts in opinion polling helps to focus the campaign on issues that have popular appeal. Much reliance is placed on persons expert in the use of media and persons knowledgeable about modern political conditions. Less dependence is placed on established political machines and political bosses in planning the grand campaign strategy. (Data from political surveys tend to support the notion that in a two-party system at least one-third of the voters are uncommitted to a party and thus are not subject to the dictates of political party machinery.[4]) Modern political campaigns are waged from detailed knowledge of demographic and socioeconomic trends that influence voting behavior. They are highly organized and efficiently run. Involved in a campaign are communication specialists, advertising agency personnel, professional pollsters, fundraising experts, intellectuals, college students, and politically active women. This is far different from a campaign built around the organizations of party ward bosses.

Literature about the new politics, like past material about voting behavior, deals largely with statewide and national elections. The most important concept that is emerging is that candidates for state and national offices are increasingly dependent on television. Many campaign managers are of the opinion that a candidate can no longer be elected to a statewide or national office unless he spends large amounts of funds on television.

The Use of Television

Mendelsohn, a mass communications researcher, has suggested that the central role played by television in modern politics is a result of "a simple-minded, primer-like logic: voter likes TV; candidate uses TV to make himself liked; voter pulls lever for 'likeable' TV candidate."[5]

There is little question that the voter likes television. Results from a 1969 poll indicated that the average American watches television

almost three hours per day. What is more important, television was the major and most believable source of news (considering national, state, and local news collectively). In response to the question of which news version the respondent would be most inclined to believe, television led newspapers two to one. However, of equal importance was the finding that in the area of local and state news the newspaper was still the main source.[6]

Candidates for national and statewide offices certainly use television. For example, in 1964, the political parties spent almost 1.5 million dollars to purchase television time from the National Broadcasting Company alone.[7] In Nelson A. Rockefeller's 1966 campaign for governor of New York, his commercials were run roughly 4,000 times on the 22 commercial television stations of that state at an estimated cost of almost 2 million dollars.[8] Television costs for his successful 1970 reelection campaign were estimated to be greater than his 1966 expenditure.[9]

In an effort to make themselves liked, many candidates for national and statewide offices hire outstanding media experts. These media men know how to promote their clients. The terms "image-making," "selling candidates," and "marketing men" are commonplace in the literature of the new politics. The object in the use of television is to package information to sell the candidate much as food product is marketed. The earlier use of television for speeches has given way to the image-makers' forms of presenting their candidates or ideas, which are designed to make a greater impact on the voters. Hill, based on his doctoral research, suggested that the great debate series between Kennedy and Nixon in the 1960 presidential campaign was one of the most dramatic techniques to be introduced. Other techniques that he found had been developed and widely applied were the documentary (combining dramatic and factual elements), the use of Hollywood personalities in spectacular productions, the spot announcement, and the five-minute "trailers" used with top-rated television network shows.[10] The point is that media experts, after intensive study, came up with a variety of packaged shows. The candidate may spend many hours "acting out" his part in these films. In some packages he may not speak or even appear, but be identified by previously established symbols. For example, in a reverse twist, during the 1964 presidential campaign, one spot announcement showed a little girl plucking flowers and an atomic explosion. These symbols were an obvious effort to exploit the trigger-happy image that had been attached to Senator Barry Goldwater.

The scene for a political presentation is not unlike the filming of a commercial show for television. The packaged material is designed to get attention and show the most favorable aspects of the candidate. Instead of a dry speech, the result is a set of very attractive packaged television shows for release at appropriate times. Sometimes an effort is made to place these packaged materials close to news broadcasts in an attempt to play down the "paid political announcement" theme. The sales package has emotional appeal. It is ideologically and symbolically impressive.

To what extent have the candidates succeeded in making themselves likable by great reliance on television? To what extent can a positive image be created? Definite answers to these questions are lacking. First, there is little evidence on the kind of image that would be most effective. If observation of the candidates in action on television is any indicator, they apparently feel that an effective image should be comprised of such characteristics as "concern," "experience," "honesty," "integrity," and "sincerity." In an empirical investigation conducted in the last five days of the 1968 Oregon presidential primary campaign, "genuineness" was found to be the most important factor, with "leadership" being important when combined with "genuineness."[11] In addition, it is methodologically difficult to isolate the impact of television from other factors that affect a candidate's image. Illustrative of the available evidence are the Rosenthal study of the persuasive effect of the 1960 Kennedy-Nixon television debates,[12] and the Benham study of the 1964 Johnson-Goldwater campaign.[13] Two of the major conclusions from the Rosenthal study were: (1) the Kennedy image, which was distinguished by positive perceptions of and reactions to intelligence and sincerity, had the greater persuasive impact, and (2) the Nixon image, which was characterized by negative perceptions of and reactions to artificiality and deception produced a lesser persuasive impact.

In 1964, both Johnson and Goldwater used television extensively. In the Benham study, 46 percent of the persons polled had seen Goldwater commercials and 39 percent had seen Johnson commercials. At the beginning of the campaign, the Johnson image was the more favorable. His image was characterized by such positive factors as "warm and friendly personality," "shows good judgment," and "progressive and forward looking." His negative image included such factors as "too much of a politician" and "promises anything to get votes." The Goldwater image was characterized by such positive

qualities as "speaks his own mind" and "has strong convictions." On the negative side Goldwater was characterized by such qualities as "acts without thinking," "too much of a politician," and "promises anything to get votes." The effects of the television-oriented campaign served to heighten most of the negative aspects and lower many of the positive qualities of the Johnson image; all of the favorable and all of the unfavorable qualities of the Goldwater image were heightened. Results from studies such as these lead to the conclusion that candidates can indeed create an image through the use of television, but unless the medium is skillfully handled it will not necessarily be a "likable image."

The ultimate question, in primer logic, is: Does the voter cast his ballot for the likable television candidate? The simple answer is "yes," based on the history of success of well-planned television campaigns, such as those conducted by John F. Kennedy, Ronald Reagan, and Nelson Rockefeller. However, a more accurate response may be that television serves to reinforce opinions and voter choices rather than to change them. In the study of the Johnson-Goldwater campaign, 79 percent of those polled did not change their voting choice between August and November, and findings from the 1960 Kennedy-Nixon election showed that 80 percent did not change their voting choice.[14] Lord Windlesham, a television executive and communications expert, in a treatise on the influence of television on political opinion noted:

Over the last two decades one of the basic findings of mass communications research has been that television is no more than one influence combining with other environmental influences and experiences to produce a total situation in which behaviour is shaped and opinions formed.[15] . . . the persuasive power of television lies not so much in conversion, since for the most part the viewer is already predisposed to accept whatever information he retains, but in reinforcement. Because there is little evidence to suggest that television converts from previous beliefs and modes of behaviour it does not follow it is ineffective. Reinforcement is an effect in itself . . . .[16]

There is little doubt that television is the major means of mass communication in the new politics. Media specialists are ingenious in designing formats to market candidates and ideas. At the very least, television has served as a reinforcing mechanism for voter opinions. However, contrary to the predictions of many, the extensive use of television has not been accompanied by great increases in the percentage of registered voters going to the polls. Voter turnout that can

be attributed directly to the effect of television has not been documented. Glaser, based on a review of a number of studies related to
the mass media and voter turnout, concluded:

When practiced jointly, newspaper reading and television watching are associated
with very high rates of turnout, but television may "add" less to the combination than newspapers.[17] . . . Television watching is closely connected with some
newspaper reading and with some personal conversations within the family, and
both of these other variables — particularly family behavior — have higher correlations with turnout than has television alone.[18]

Massive Use of Money

Campaigning is becoming increasingly expensive. The total cost of
all elections was estimated at roughly 175 million dollars in 1960,
200 million in 1964, and 250 million in 1968.[19] Obviously inflation
and an increased voter population have contributed to the rising
costs of political campaigns; however, a major factor is the use of
television, which is very expensive. The October 1970 *Newsweek*
article on the use of television in elections reported that media men
who package the image-building material and market the candidate
commanded fees of $100,000 and more. Some demand 15 percent of
the total campaign chest for their services. Conservative estimates
placed expenditures by the presidential, gubernatorial, and senatorial
candidates for air time in the 1968 elections at almost 60 million
dollars. When the cost of producing the films and tapes is included,
the total comes close to 90 million dollars.[20] Baus and Ross compared political campaigning to tossing a salad consisting of money
and men.[21]

Television is, of course, not the only cost in running a modern
campaign. White's discussion of the Kennedy technique in the Wis-
consin and West Virginia primaries emphasized the large number of
campaign workers.[22] Even though many of these workers were not
paid a salary, their travel and per diem expenses alone would be
sizable. The candidate must either own or rent a private airplane. He
must have the ready advice of campaign strategists and polling experts. Consequently, even without the high cost of television, the
new politics is no place for a poor man. Indeed, many are saying
that only the rich can participate as candidates. The poor man
running for statewide or national office has no alternative but to turn
to rich economic interests for funds. Thus he runs the risk of being
an "owned" officeholder.

The need for massive amounts of money has led to a number of fundraising techniques, including dinners, dances, and the like; direct solicitation from selected wealthy persons; regular contributions from the "little man"; the assignment of quotas to state and local political party committees; and appeals for funds via television, radio, and newspapers. This need has also brought an important participant to the new politics — the professional fundraiser.

The Campaign Strategy

In a modern presidential campaign, the candidate is made or broken on the grand campaign strategy he constructs following the nominating conventions. This is nothing new, and it is not easy to say how the new politics have changed the game from previous election campaigns. Some would contend that in the new politics the planning of the grand strategy is based on more political expertise and scientific data than were the campaigns of yesteryear. For example, public opinion polling is a vital support for today's campaigns.

As the masterminds for a presidential candidate look at the United States, they must decide areas of concentration that will assure victory. For example, the popular press placed great significance on the "Southern strategy" reported to have been developed by Richard Nixon's brain trust during his successful 1968 campaign for the presidency. The results of public opinion polls figure heavily in the campaign decisions. Campaign scheduling is tremendously risky. The schedule must provide the right amounts of time for each stop and proceed efficiently. Advance men must prepare the candidate's visit. The campaign requires speechwriters, media experts, polling experts, and numerous persons to perform organizational details.

Among those who prepare the grand strategy must be persons who have had direct experience in national campaigns for the presidency. There must also be persons who qualify as political tacticians and as political organizers. Intellectuals are needed to furnish ideas. The group must include logistics managers, media experts, and persons experienced in partisan politics.

The actual organization of workers and leaders for the campaign is based on directions incorporated in the grand strategy. The organization must be expanded and expanded until campaign leaders and workers cover all major population areas considered to be significant in the grand strategy. In some respects the new politics is different

from the old politics in that its success is not entirely dependent upon existing political leaders in the far-flung communities of the nation. Many campaign workers may not have been active in politics before; this was true of many who worked in campaigns for the late Senator Estes Kefauver of Tennessee and for Senator Eugene McCarthy of Minnesota in his 1968 presidential bid. Thus, the new politics may skillfully activate the latent power interests of the power structures. (The concept of latent centers of power was discussed in Chapter 2.)

Modern campaigning is different from earlier politics in that public opinion polling allows the campaign strategists to determine which issues are most important in different areas of the nation. The polls show how intensively different population areas feel about these issues. Thus, the candidate no longer has to make "best guesses" concerning the dynamics of political issues.

Use of Professional Agencies

As the reader can appreciate, managing a campaign for statewide or national office has become very complex. Therefore, many candidates have not attempted to run their own campaigns, but have turned to professional campaign organizers. These agencies have in the past largely restricted their operations to the management of communications and fundraising. In the future, however, we may well see a professionalization of politics through the campaign agencies.

Usefulness of New Politics Techniques to Educators

In order to discuss the new politics, the previous section had to emphasize statewide and national elections. These are where the new politics have been used. There has been little use of the new politics in local elections. The significant question for educators is how applicable the new politics may be for school elections restricted to the voters in a local school district.

In previous chapters, the authors have already emphasized the usefulness of many techniques used in the new politics, such as careful attention to campaign strategy and the use of opinion polling. The critical questions still to be answered concern the use of television, campaign funds, and the use of professional agencies in school elec-

tions. The relative merits of these aspects of the new politics for educational elections are discussed below.

Television in School Elections

In reviewing the literature the authors found little definitive evidence concerning the influence of the new politics, and particularly television, on voter behavior. If scientific studies show that campaigning by television does make the marketing concept viable, the earlier opinion leader concept of Lazarsfeld and associates[23] (see Chapter 3) may need to be revised. Perhaps candidates and education proposals can really be sold via television much as soap, toys, and pet food are marketed. However, data on the actual impact of television are far from conclusive, except in saying that television does serve to reinforce previously held opinions.

The case for television is largely impressionistic. For instance, much was made of the 1970 Ohio Democratic primary race for the United States Senate, in which a virtually unknown millionaire (Howard Metzenbaum) defeated a national hero (John Glenn). Observers believed large expenditures for television time by the unknown made the difference. Certainly this is plausible under the circumstances. However, the same media agent who managed the winner's campaign in that Ohio primary election managed the loser's campaign in the 1970 Republican primary for the governorship of Florida. The agent's client in Florida was a wealthy businessman who also spent much money on packaged television time. His opponent, the incumbent and a well-entrenched politician, spent very little on television. Further, in the 1970 regular election in Ohio, Mr. Metzenbaum was defeated by a narrow margin by his Republican opponent, Robert Taft, Jr. Mr. Taft was an experienced politician with the added advantage of a political heritage dating back many generations.

At this writing we are too close to the emergence of television as a political tool to assess scientifically how it will ultimately influence campaigns. The television industry and media experts have led many to believe television is "everything." There is strong belief among many that candidates must develop good acting ability. Wyckoff expresses the opinion that what the politician says is less important than what the viewer sees.[24] He has even suggested that future presidential candidates will be made or broken by the impression they make on the television audience.

Some authors have produced evidence indicating that television may not have the striking influence claimed by its proponents. In Glaser's study of relationships between the media and voter turnout, the findings were somewhat inconclusive about the effectiveness of television.[25] Some writers have contended that television is only one of many influences on public opinion. Anderson suggested that the advantages of television will be canceled out because all major candidates for office will employ good media agencies.[26] Furthermore, he did not feel that television will submerge the campaign issues. According to many observers of the 1970 regular elections, candidates who relied almost exclusively on television campaigns were generally not successful.

Some authorities have expressed the view that television may not be as important for local elections as for state and national elections. Indeed, there is some evidence that newspapers and perhaps radio may have more impact in local elections than television. Thus, schoolmen in many districts may find that the use of television is not practical or that other media have greater impact for local school elections.

In promoting educational proposals in statewide elections, television could certainly be used to advantage. Voters are frequently asked to approve changes in the state constitution that will be beneficial to educational development. In addition, the legislature will frequently approve school-related bills subject to a state referendum. For example, the legislature may adopt a tax subject to referendum, and the outcome could mean the loss or gain of many millions of dollars for schools. Thus, educators are called upon to furnish leadership in statewide campaigns when the outcomes will be of great importance for education in the state. Educational leaders should use modern political techniques, including television, in these campaigns.

If school leaders learn from the experts, they will use attractively packaged material (e.g., the documentary, spot announcement, and five-minute trailer), avoid drab, boring lectures, and stifle the urge to pontificate. Television is too important a resource to be overlooked in conducting school elections. However, educators may need to seek donated time in many instances, because the commercial use of television is very expensive.

Large Expenditures of Funds

There are two very important questions about the amount of money involved in the new politics and educational elections. Can educational leaders raise the amount of money involved? If large sums are spent on media packages and campaign agencies, what will be the effect on voters? These questions cannot be answered through scientific evidence. The reader must make his own judgment in terms of his school district and his other campaign alternatives.

The authors have emphasized throughout that education leaders must use sound political techniques in designing their campaign strategy. This strategy must be based on the conditions existing in the district (e.g., public opinion, power structure, socioeconomic status). Obviously, the new politics becomes more necessary as the school district grows in population. For example, educators, with the help of professionals, could raise the money, develop "slick" television packages, and use these packages extensively in a school election in a city the size of New York, Chicago, or Los Angeles. On the other hand an expensively run modern campaign in an Iowa school district could backfire and result in defeat of the school proposal. The positive impression of the campaign might be offset by voter perception and resentment of pressure from a "big money" campaign.

The authors are of the opinion that rather extensive expenditures are usually essential for campaign success in school districts of above 75,000 enrollment. We are also aware that schoolmen may run an excellent, new politics type of campaign with very few dollars, by working with leaders in the local power structure to obtain donations of media services and other services in kind. This approach may be the most feasible way to finance modern campaigns in most school districts. In the illustrative campaign described in Chapter 7, several examples are offered dealing with fundraising, donated media services, and services in kind.

Use of Professional Agencies

To what extent should school officials rely on professional agencies to run their campaigns? There is no research evidence concerning the consequences of employing an outside agency to organize and run campaigns in local school districts. In one local school district known to the authors, educational leaders contracted with an agency that in effect ran the successful campaign. However, it is unclear how

successful this approach might be if used in other school districts with widely varying conditions. Legal difficulties might be encountered in some states. Citizen backlash to the outside agency is obviously an important consideration.

Since there is no well-documented research on the use of outside agencies, schoolmen must observe prudence in deciding how these agencies may assist in campaigns. In many school districts the leaders will have to rely on outside resources for various aspects of the campaign. For example, many school districts do not have anyone with the expertise necessary to take a public opinion poll. Even the larger districts with the expertise for an in-house poll should consider using outside inputs to assure an unbiased poll. The central question, however, is how schoolmen should use campaign management agencies.

The widespread use of agencies to organize and actually conduct campaigns might have some negative long term consequences. The authors emphasized in previous chapters the importance of schoolmen achieving leadership among the citizens of the school district and the significance of effective school public relations as a basis for successful school elections. Studies of voting behavior show clearly that many people decide very early how they will vote. The way they vote depends upon their favorable or unfavorable dispositions toward the schools, education leaders, and other considerations. If schoolmen rely entirely on agencies, they may become further removed from the citizenry, creating a greater possibility of credibility gaps, poor school public relations, and negative attitudes about schools developing among citizens.

This is not to say that local school district leaders may not prudently use outside agencies. They should be used, but not used continuously as a "crutch" to compensate for lack of leadership in the community.

What constitutes prudent use of the agencies will depend upon local conditions. There are at least three possible relationships between the school board and outside agencies: The outside agency may be put in charge of running the campaign, it may provide advice and services to local school officials who are in charge of the campaign, or it may be largely advisory to the school leaders. While conditions might dictate active participation of agency personnel in conducting the campaign, the most likely and probably the most prudent use is to employ agency personnel in an advisory and service

relationship, leaving the actual, visible conduct of the campaign to local lay and school leaders. Thus, agencies may provide a direct service in conducting polls, packaging television commercials, designing posters, and preparing other materials. The agency may provide advice to local school leaders in organizing and conducting the campaign. The visible leadership (i.e., those who give talks, organize the campaign workers, etc.) in the campaign should be drawn from lay leaders, board members, professional educators, and other citizens.

Suggested Readings

Baus, Herbert M., and William B. Ross. *Politics Battle Plan*. New York: Macmillan Company, 1968.

Kinter, Robert E. "Television and the World of Politics," *Harper's*, vol. 230, no. 1380 (May 1965), pp. 121–32.

McGinnis, Joe. *The Selling of the President 1968*. New York: Trident Press, 1969.

Mendelsohn, Harold. "A New Style for Politics," *Nation*, vol. 202, no. 23 (June 6, 1966), pp. 669–73.

White, Theodore H. *The Making of the President 1960*. New York: New American Library, 1961.

———. *The Making of the President 1964*. New York: New American Library, 1965.

Wilson, Roy K. "Are Madison Avenue Public Relations Techniques Good Enough for the Schools?" *National Association of Secondary School Principals Bulletin*, vol. 48, no. 291 (April 1964), pp. 76–89.

Windlesham, Lord. "Television as an Influence on Public Opinion," *Political Quarterly*, vol. 35, no. 1 (January-March 1964), pp. 375–85.

Wyckoff, Gene. *The Image Candidates: American Politics in the Age of Television*. New York: Macmillan Company, 1968.

Footnotes

1. Robert L. Crain, Elihu Katz, and Donald B. Rosenthal, *The Politics of Community Conflict: The Fluoridation Decision* (New York: Bobbs-Merrill Company, 1969).

2. Karl E. Meyer, "Mirror, Mirror...," *New Statesman*, vol. 67, no. 1713 (January 10, 1964), pp. 33–34.

3. Theodore H. White, *The Making of the President 1960* (New York: New American Library, 1961).

4. Mark Abrams, "Opinion Polls and Party Propaganda," *Public Opinion Quarterly*, vol. 28, no. 1 (Spring 1964), pp. 13—19.

5. Harold Mendelsohn, "A New Style for Politics," *Nation*, vol. 202, no. 23 (June 6, 1966), p. 670.

6. Richard L. Tobin, "Our Basic News Medium," *Saturday Review*, vol. 52, no. 32 (August 9, 1969), pp. 41—42.

7. Robert E. Kintner, "Television and the World of Politics," *Harper's*, vol. 230, no. 1380 (May 1965), p. 126.

8. James M. Perry, "This Rockefeller Campaign Is the Biggest, Maybe Best," *National Observer*, vol. 9, no. 43 (October 26, 1970), p. 13.

9. "The Selling of the Candidates," *Newsweek*, vol. 76, no. 16 (October 19, 1970), p. 34.

10. Ruane B. Hill, "Political Uses of Broadcasting in the United States in the Context of Public Opinion and the Political Process, 1920—1960." (doctoral thesis, Northwestern University, 1964).

11. Bill O. Kjeldahl, "Factors in a Presidential Candidate's Image" (doctoral thesis, University of Oregon, 1969).

12. Paul I. Rosenthal, "Ethos in the Presidential Campaign of 1960: A Study of the Basic Persuasive Process of the Kennedy-Nixon Television Debates" (doctoral thesis, University of California at Los Angeles, 1963).

13. Thomas W. Benham, "Polling for a Presidential Candidate: Some Observations on the 1964 Campaign," *Public Opinion Quarterly*, vol. 29, no. 2 (Summer 1965), pp. 185—99.

14. *Ibid.*

15. Lord Windlesham, "Television as an Influence on Political Opinion," *Political Quarterly*, vol. 35, no. 1 (January-March 1964), p. 376.

16. *Ibid.*, p. 377.

17. William A. Glaser, "Television and Voting Turnout," *Public Opinion Quarterly*, vol. 29, no. 1 (Spring 1965), p. 85.

18. *Ibid.*, p. 86.

19. "What It All Cost," *Economist*, vol. 229, no. 6533 (November 9, 1968), p. 32.

20. "The Selling of the Candidates," *loc. cit.*

21. Herbert M. Baus and William B. Ross, *Politics Battle Plan* (New York: Macmillan Company, 1968).

22. White, *loc. cit.*

23. Paul F. Lazarsfeld, Bernard R. Berelson, and Hazel Gaudet, *The People's Choice* (New York: Columbia University Press, 1948).

24. Gene Wyckoff, *The Image Candidates: American Politics in the Age of Television* (New York: Macmilllan Company, 1968).

25. Glaser, *op. cit.*, pp. 71—86.

26. Patrick Anderson, "Issues Versus Image," *New Republic*, vol. 158, no. 17, (April 27, 1968), pp. 32—35.

7

A Referendum
in Cape City

The authors considered various approaches for illustrating how the concepts presented in the preceding chapters should be used in political campaigns. We thought of offering several cases with descriptions of planned campaigns for each, but there are so many alternative campaign strategies possible for many school districts that an attempt to describe several cases in depth would run into volumes. Consequently, we decided to review one case in some detail.

The local district serving as the illustration for demonstrating a political strategy is given the fictitious name, Cape City. Two bond elections were held in the district during a four-year period; the first was defeated and the second passed.

In describing the political strategy used in the winning campaign, the authors have added some techniques that were not used in the actual case, in order to illustrate better how a good campaign ideally should be run. The major addition was the use of public opinion polls. Except for this, most of the descriptions follow the actual strategy used.

Characteristics of Cape City

Cape City is a large industrial city located on a coastal area of the United States. At the time of the campaign, the Cape City school system enrolled about 70,000 pupils, and the enrollment was increasing each year. The non-public-school enrollment included about 7 percent of the school age population. Two universities (one public and one private) were located within the city. Several large suburban communities had developed near the core city. Room for the city to expand was limited. While Cape City was usually referred to as an

industrial area, it also had sizable port facilities and other commercial developments. Several large national corporations had branch operations in the city. It was an important trade and financial center for a large area of the state. Tourism was also an important part of the economic system. There was the usual array of cultural and recreational opportunities, including a "struggling" art center, a civic center, and a relatively new athletic stadium.

Cape City had the population characteristics usually associated with cities. There was a large Spanish-speaking population that had traditionally been a close-knit ethnic group. A large black population (roughly 30 percent of the total) was concentrated in the downtown areas. There had been some shifting of the white middle class residents to suburban areas as the immigrant population grew in numbers and percentage of the total population. Considerable poverty was manifest among the families of the slum areas. The only unusual factor in the age distribution of the population was the fact that roughly 15 percent were in the over 65 category.

About 38 percent of the population was in the work force. Unemployment approximated the national rate with much higher percentages among the undereducated minority groups. Consistent with the economic base of the community, the occupational groups that predominated included the professional, managerial, and technical groups; the clerical and sales groups; the service groups; and the skilled and semi-skilled worker groups. Average family income was slightly below the national average.

In supporting its public services and institutions, Cape City, like most other cities, depended upon a combination of federal, state, and local funds. The local funds were derived chiefly from a general property tax and consumer taxes (the retail sales tax was the biggest revenue producer). The bonded indebtedness of the city equaled about 10 percent of the assessed value of real property.

The city was served by large circulation morning and afternoon dailies (the *Cape City Post* and the *Coast Chronicle*). A small Spanish-language daily served the Spanish-speaking groups. Three television stations (WCAP, WCOS, and WCIT), each with a national network affiliation, and five radio stations (one catering to the black community and one a Spanish-language station) were located in the city.

The Need for a Bond Election

The bond election in Cape City provides an excellent illustration of a successful election campaign in a city with a history of hostility to additional bonding authority for the public schools. The campaign described here followed an unsuccessful bond election two years earlier, in which the school officials relied on techniques that were not tailored to the realities of the political system. Seven years before that defeat a bond proposed by the board of education had also been defeated by the voters.

As a result of voter resistance to bonding authority, school building needs were critical. Almost 20 percent of the pupils were on half-day sessions and another 25 percent were attending school in substandard classrooms. In addition, estimates indicated that the school enrollment was expected to increase by about 10 percent during the next two years. Local school officials described the situation as a "20-year backlog of school construction needs."

The Political System

At the time of the bond election described here, the political system in Cape City was characterized by low conflict and monolithic control by very powerful men. Professionals, businessmen, elected public officials, and retired persons were among the influentials of the political system. The decisionmaking process in the system was heavily influenced by businessmen, such as bankers, retail merchants, industrialists, corporation executives, wealthy attorneys, food processors, realtors, newspapermen, and other prominent leaders in the economic system.

For example, one of the most powerful men in the system was Bert Saunders, Chairman of the Board of the First National Bank and Trust Company. Mr. Saunders had very extensive influence among loan companies, merchants, and other business leaders of Cape City. He was ably represented by the law firm of Lankston, Landry, Strateymer, and Sorenson. Mr. Saunders had lived in Cape City all his life and had had a very big hand in the economic growth of the area. He had a following throughout Cape City based on longtime personal friendship and various business connections. He was known as a moderately conservative person in his attitudes toward economic and public development.

Another very influential leader in Cape City was Rayfield S. Spears, President of General Steel Corporation. Mr. Spears also had extensive holdings in other national corporations and in various business enterprises in Cape City. For instance, he was a big stockholder and a member of the board of directors of International Aircraft Corporation. He was instrumental in helping the governor stall a proposal by International Aircraft to locate a plant in a nearby state. He was very concerned that the lack of vocational and technical training schools placed Cape City in a poor bargaining position to compete with other cities for the aircraft plant. Spears was also a member of the board of directors of the First National Bank and Trust Company.

Senator Roger Sorenson, a member of the law firm Lankston, Landry, Strateymer, and Sorenson, was widely recognized as one of the most effective politicians in the state legislature. In fact, he had been recently reelected to the state legislature by the biggest plurality ever registered by a candidate in his district. Sorenson had a keen intellect. One often heard accounts of how he could maneuver to pass bills he favored and scuttle those he opposed. In some instances he had criticized the organization and administration of the public schools in the state. He had also singled out the Cape City Schools for some criticism.

Saunders, Spears, and Sorenson were but three of about 40 or 50 persons who could be identified as influential in the power structure of Cape City. For example, any discussion of politics would be incomplete without mention of James Hall, the oldest politician in years of service in the county courthouse for Cape County. Mention should also be made of Mayor Vasquez Luicquo who had recently emerged to political importance in the city. The names of many prominent businessmen would be included such as Fred Jenkins, a realtor, and Buck Pendergrast, a fuel oil distributor.

There was definitely a hierarchy of influence among the influentials of the power structure. At the top levels of the hierarchy were very prominent businessmen and public officials who were longtime residents of Cape City. The structure was resistant to the emergence of newcomers to Cape City into positions of prominence.

The Democratic Party was predominant in partisan politics in the city, although the Republican Party gave a very good account of itself in state and national elections because many of the middle class, white-collar, suburban areas were solidly Republican.

The Cape City political system had a history of conservatism. The influentials' attitudes toward the public schools might best be described as satisfied indifference. They had limited contact with school officials and, as a consequence, no firsthand knowledge about the critical needs of schools. In private conversation they expressed general satisfaction with the school system.

Preparing for the Campaign

Key leaders in the central administrative staff of the Cape City school system spent much time in informal discussion about the need for a bond referendum. From this discussion emerged the realization that the previous campaign had been poorly planned. The school executives also realized that future campaigns would have to be very carefully planned to be successful.

Studying the Previous Campaign and Results

Preparation for the election campaign began with what Mr. Glenn Rickert, Superintendent of Schools in Cape City, described as a "postmortem" concerning the reason for the failure of the bond election two years earlier. Superintendent Rickert and his staff were greatly disappointed over the fact that their previous efforts had resulted in a 2-to-1 defeat of the bond proposal. They spent days in conference discussing why the earlier campaign had failed. The group attempted to organize a complete history of the previous campaign.

The election statistics were analyzed. Interviews were conducted with leaders in precincts voting heavily against the school bonding proposal. Newspapers and other documentary evidence were studied. The methods used in the campaign were analyzed to discover their impact on voters. Several outside consultants assisted in the analysis and development of observations about the failure of the bond proposal.

The group sought answers to many questions about the previous campaign, including these: What percentage of the eligible voters participated? What were the patterns of voting in precincts? What were the sources of voter resistance? Who were the leaders in the campaign? Was there evidence of changes in voter opinion during the campaign? What were the significant sources of voter behavior in the campaign? What were the consequences of techniques employed by

school leaders? What changes in basic strategies might have produced a majority in favor of the school proposal?

Superintendent Rickert and his associates discovered several important errors that they had made in the previous campaign. They had not compiled enough factual material to demonstrate school needs. Public opinion polls, which could have provided information for better planning, had not been conducted. The material prepared for release by the mass media was not attractive. Their campaign was not well organized. They did not use some important grassroots techniques that would have been helpful.

Perhaps the most revealing weakness in the earlier strategy, however, was that the schoolmen had ignored the influentials in the power structure. The campaign had been based on an oversimplified grassroots approach. Consequently, school officials decided to make very significant changes in their basic strategy for the upcoming campaign.

Developing the Data Base and Board Support

As a second step in preparing for the campaign, Superintendent Rickert and his staff decided that a thorough review of the data was in order, even though it probably meant documenting the obvious. A seven-man outside team, which included representatives from the state department of education and a state university, was called in to (1) analyze existing buildings for structural and educational adequacy, (2) review available demographic data and compute another set of enrollment estimates, (3) study building use and pupil attendance zones, and (4) examine the financial resources of the district.

During the 60 days of the study process, key members of the professional establishment and the Cape City Board of Education were kept informed and their judgments sought. Superintendent Rickert considered board involvement to be essential because Mr. James X. White, a newly elected board member and a champion of the poor, felt that a bond issue would, as he expressed it, "hurt my people" and, besides, "buildings don't make a school."

As a result of the study and deliberations, one new senior high school facility, two new junior high schools, and nine new elementary schools were recommended, along with appropriate locations. Remodeling and additions were recommended for over 30 existing

buildings. The financial data clearly demonstrated that the only possible way under existing state law to provide the facilities and improvements was by means of a bond issue. The amount needed was estimated at $30,000,000.

The recommendations were supported by the staff and the entire Board of Education, including the reluctant Mr. White, who admitted himself that he had not really understood the urgency of the situation until he participated in the study. He was particularly shocked at the crowded and rundown conditions of the buildings serving poor people.

The First Poll

The first formal opinion poll in preparation for the campaign was conducted during March 1968. A proportional systematic sample was chosen from each voting precinct (the latest registered voter list was used to draw the sample), and 362 persons were interviewed. The team of 20 interviewers was selected locally. Care was taken not to use persons identified with the school system. The results indicated only limited knowledge about the crowded and obsolete facilities and substantial opposition to a bonding proposal at that time. However, the poll also indicated a large number of voters who were undecided. There was much resistance to a bond proposal in some precincts in the "Spanish-speaking" areas of town and in areas where the previously proposed new school construction would have promoted more racial desegregation. The poll indicated that many people who were favorable to the previous bond proposal had not voted.

The large "undecided" vote was an optimistic sign to Superintendent Rickert's group. If they could be assured of winning a majority of this vote and could secure the active participation of those favoring the proposal who had not voted in the previous campaign, there was a very good chance of passing the proposal.

Involving the Influentials

Superintendent Rickert expressed one change of tactics in the campaign as follows:

The pitfalls of the unsuccessful elections were analyzed and resulted in a decision to go directly to the controlling powers in town. Accordingly, school officials approached several prominent citizens, recognized leaders of the communi-

ty, to ask whether they would be willing to hear the school story and evaluate the facts.

After making personal contacts with many of the key influentials of the power structure, the school officials were encouraged to organize a meeting. Of some interest was the insistence of the influentials not to make the meeting public at that point. It was held in the offices of the General Steel Corporation with Mr. Rayfield S. Spears acting somewhat as host to the group. Some 20 opinion leaders attended. Mr. Rickert and his staff presented all the evidence at their disposal, including a review of the hard data and recommendations of the outside study team. Several members of the Board of Education, including Mr. White, assisted in presenting the data and recommendations. The school officials solicited the assistance of the influentials in promoting a bond issue. The only firm agreement that was reached was to meet again one week later in the same place. This arrangement obviously gave the influentials an opportunity to "check around" and consider their position carefully.

After considerable eyeball-to-eyeball discussion at the second meeting, the group agreed to support the passage of a bonding proposal. There was much less agreement on the amount of bonding authority to be sought. Superintendent Rickert and the Board of Education felt that they had a justified need for more bonding authority than many of the influentials felt necessary. Agreement was finally reached to support a slightly smaller bond issue ($25,000,000 as opposed to the $30,000,000 recommended), with the stipulation that the group would give full support to another bond issue if conditions justified one within the next four or five years. There was some reason to believe that the state legislature would increase funds for school construction in its upcoming session.

It would be inaccurate to imply that all of the influentials in the power structure favored the bonding proposal. Several key leaders did not show up at the meetings. For example, Mr. Saunders, Chairman of the First National Bank and Trust Company, was insistent that a bond issue was not needed. Through a long process of personal interaction with him, Mr. Jerome Jacobs, Chairman of the Board of Education, succeeded in getting a commitment from Mr. Saunders that he would not actively oppose the bonding authority. As Mr. Saunders stated it, "I won't oppose you in it, but I will not help you either." He later changed his position and supported the bond issue.

In several instances, including the negotiations with Mr. Saunders, influentials supporting the proposal obtained the assistance of nationally prominent businessmen outside Cape City to "reason with those in opposition to the board proposal." In fact, it was just such a person who was credited with moving Mr. Saunders from his position of neutrality to one of support for the school proposal.

Impact of the Influentials

It is significant that much of the dynamics of power exercised here occurred before public announcement of plans to seek bonding authority. Yet, this was a very important part of the political activity designed to have a favorable impact on public opinion. Leadership activity following the informal meetings produced some immediately observable results favorable to the schools. The actions of the influentials served to open the political system to the use of other techniques for promoting the school proposal.

For instance, organizational resistance experienced in the first bond issue turned to one of open support and assistance. Over 70 organizations endorsed the school bond proposal before the campaign was completed. The newspapers came out strongly in support. Television and radio time was made available to lay and professional leaders supporting school bonding. In fact, Superintendent Rickert stated that the support of influentials was "a tremendous factor in the bond issue passage."

However, the bond issue would have certainly failed again if the school officials had relied entirely upon support of the influentials. In a real sense, the influentials functioned to open resources for the educators to use in carrying the total campaign strategy to the people. Thus, the school officials had succeeded in opening the power structure for effective community participation.

Organizing and Conducting the Campaign

According to Superintendent Rickert, the bond election would not have been successful without a well-organized campaign. Thousands of man-hours were invested in organizing the grassroots phase of the campaign strategy.

Organizing the Citizens

One outcome of the early informal meetings with Cape City influentials was a decision by the Board of Education to appoint a Citizens' Advisory Committee. Several of the influentials most actively motivated for the school proposal were appointed to the 50-member committee. However, the membership was expanded to include opinion leaders from throughout Cape City. Rayfield S. Spears, who had demonstrated a growing interest in the schools, was appointed chairman of the committee. This committee played a prominent part in promoting the bond issue. Announcement by press, television, and radio of the creation and membership of this Citizens' Advisory Committee was made in July 1968 only 48 hours after public notification of the bond referendum to be held on November 5, 1968.

As a first move the Citizens' Advisory Committee agreed to assume direct responsibility for financing the campaign. A three-member group, headed by "Doc" Scott, a well-known local druggist, was assigned to raise the money. Scott was ably assisted by Mrs. J. Wentworth Hoozier, a prominent local clubwoman (her deceased husband had headed a large wholesaling operation in Cape City), and Louis B. Quinton, past head of a large local union. This group succeeded in raising the needed money or "services in kind." For example, a benefit dance sponsored by Mrs. Hoozier at the Buckhills Country Club raised several thousand dollars. Neighborhood coffees raised several hundred dollars. Direct solicitations in the business community and industrial plants produced more money. Contributed services in kind included free printing of a fact sheet by a local printer, newspaper ads donated by individuals and firms, postage paid for by a local beverage dealer, and use of a downtown store building for the committee headquarters contributed by a large real estate firm.

The second major step taken by the Citizens' Advisory Committee was the formation of a Publicity Advisory Board and a Speakers' Bureau. The Publicity Advisory Board was chaired by B. Carl Haynes, Director of Public Information for International Aircraft. Dr. Vincent M. Moffett, Vice President for Development, Cape City State University, assumed responsibility for the Speakers' Bureau.

The third major organizational step taken by the Advisory Committee was to develop a technique for voter contact. "Football teams" were formed under the leadership of Mr. L. M. Monteze, a well-known local automobile dealer, and Mrs. Dewey Gillam, the

wife of a local food processor and mother of "Bull" Gillam — a widely celebrated star of one of the local high school football teams. Eleven persons in different sectors of the city were asked to "captain" teams and to secure 10 other persons for their team. These team members were, in turn, each asked to secure 10 other team members and form other teams. This "chain letter" process resulted in voter contact teams being formed for practically every neighborhood in Cape City.

Organizing the Professional Establishment

As an outgrowth of the second private meeting of the influentials, a decision was made that the educators would confine themselves to supporting activities and leave the visible leadership to the lay citizens. Obviously, Superintendent Rickert and members of his immediate staff consulted frequently with the citizen leaders; other organizational liaisons and advisory arrangements were also made. For example, to work with B. Carl Haynes and the Publicity Advisory Board, a group of administrators and teachers was assigned the task of pulling together data and providing first drafts of major pieces of campaign literature. School personnel were assigned to act as research consultants to each lay speaker from the Speakers' Bureau. PTA mothers were organized for a telephone campaign. The school district's clerical staff was organized to assist in this process by helping to answer technical questions and by addressing envelopes to those who requested more information as a result of the telephone contact.

A general request for volunteers from the school district "family" was made by Mr. Spears. This resulted in over 300 additional members of the educational establishment being available on an "as the need arises" basis. Most of these persons performed in a supporting capacity at some point during the campaign. Their activities included envelope stuffing, checking voter registration lists, and distributing campaign literature at various public gatherings (e.g., football games, political rallies, civic functions, and labor meetings).

Campaign Literature

Four major pieces of campaign literature were developed and printed for wide public distribution. One of these was a one-page leaflet

printed on both front and back. It was entitled "A Challenge," and its basic theme was "Our Children Depend Upon Us to Provide Adequate Schools." This leaflet contained information about the number of children on half-day sessions, the number in substandard classrooms, the number of additional children expected in the fall of 1969 and the fall of 1970, the dates and locations for voter re-registration, the total amount of the bond issue and method of retirement, and a detailed listing of what uses would be made of the funds.

The second leaflet (also one page and printed front and back) was "Cape City Schools' Budget in Brief." This was a fact sheet showing the sources of revenue for the schools from each governmental level and how the money was being spent during the 1968–1969 school year.

The third publicity leaflet featured endorsements by prominent local groups with the caption, "They Care for Our Children." The leaflet also showed a sample marked ballot and a breakdown of the annual and weekly cost to a taxpaper based on his previous year's taxes.

The fourth major piece of literature was a "foldout" designed to fit in a number 10 envelope. The cover contained the picture of a single child. Above the child was the heading, "Let's Face It in 1968" and beneath the child was the simple question, "Will there be room for me?" This pamphlet, which made extensive use of pictures and light and dark typefaces of varying sizes, told the complete story of the bond issue.

Each piece of literature noted in a prominent spot that it was prepared and paid for by the Citizens' Advisory Committee, Rayfield S. Spears, Chairman. In response to a widespread fear that had developed among large segments of the voting public, each piece of literature also stated that passage of the bond issue would in no way endanger certain taxpayers' exemptions under the state constitution.

In addition to the major pieces of literature, several mimeographed handouts were prepared for group meetings. These included a general information sheet about the Cape City schools, a question and answer handout, a response to opposition questions, and a handout making a series of financial comparisons between the Cape City schools and neighboring districts.

Distribution of Information

In distributing campaign information a variety of techniques were used and a number of opportunities presented themselves. At each of the over 400 speeches made by Dr. Moffett's 150-member Speakers' Bureau, literature was distributed. Some 15,000 homes were contacted by the "football teams" organized by Mr. Monteze and Mrs. Gillam, and each was provided literature. The PTA mothers' telephone campaign resulted in over 7,500 contacts; each person requesting written information received it. Each of the over 1,500 persons who called or wrote in response to television and radio spot announcements received the information requested. Literature was also distributed at PTA meetings, football games, labor meetings, civic meetings, coffee and coke parties, and political rallies. The bond referendum was held at the same time as a general presidential election. Thus, political rallies provided a frequent opportunity to distribute information (several state and national candidates were in Cape City at some time during the campaign).

The school system's message was also disseminated by means of newspaper ads, television and radio spots, ten well-placed billboard ads, and placards in the windows of local retail establishments.

The Role of the Mass Media

Some observers might say that the bond referendum campaign in Cape City was assured of success when no major opposition materialized from the press, television, or radio. The astute analyst would be compelled to note that the low level of organized opposition may have been a result of "behind the scenes" work on the part of key influentials and continued contact with editors and owners of the media by Superintendent Rickert and his staff.

Mr. McGill Patterson, Editor of the *Cape City Post* and a close friend of Mr. Spears, gave strong editorial support almost immediately after Mr. Spears accepted the chairmanship of the Citizens' Advisory Committee. The *Cape City Post* performed another very important service by running a series of stories about the district and its problems emphasizing that the bond issue and the desegregation issue were different matters. Mr. Spray Warren, a prominent businessman, and his "local control" group were striving to make the point that a vote for the bond issue was a "vote for integration."

Editorially, the *Coast Chronicle* was noncommittal until late September at which time it endorsed the district's proposal. The *Coast Chronicle* had long been a strong supporter of Senator Roger Sorenson. Senator Sorenson and Bert Saunders were longtime close associates. As mentioned previously, Mr. Jacobs, Chairman of the Board of Education, succeeded in getting Mr. Saunders to take first a neutral position, and later one of support. When Saunders shifted his position, he in turn moved the senator from a "wait and see" position to one of open support. The senator's efforts and those of Mr. Jacobs then resulted in the endorsement of the *Chronicle*, with a strong supporting editorial.

The Spanish-language paper endorsed the proposal early in the campaign primarily as a result of the work of Mr. Monteze. All papers provided full and fair coverage of the news events associated with the campaign, and all accepted both pro-proposal ads and opposition ads.

The three television stations ran spot announcements and, as described later, donated some prime time. The assistance of a person skilled in packaging material for television was secured to aid in preparing the spot announcements. Station WCAP also gave strong endorsement in its five-minute personal opinion program, following the early evening local news.

The radio stations, with one exception, also provided spot time and donated time for panel discussions and debates on the issue. The management of radio station WTXC (Spray Warren was the majority stockholder in the station) opposed the bond issue vigorously and provided a platform for the opposition forces.

Public Endorsements

The public endorsements of the district's bond proposal began in a modest manner. However, as a result of the diligence of Mr. Spears, other influentials who were members of the Citizens' Advisory Committee, Superintendent Rickert, other members of the Cape City schools staff, and members of the Board of Education, the public endorsement campaign soon built until, as Superintendent Rickert put it, "It was the popular thing to do." More than 70 organizations and groups eventually endorsed the bond issue. These groups permitted use of their names in campaign literature, and several purchased time or space from the local media to endorse the issue. In addition

to the influentials who served as members of the Citizens' Advisory Committee, several other opinion leaders publicly supported the proposal. These included Mr. Bert Saunders.

The group endorsements represented a wide variety of interests within Cape City, including the Cape City Merchants' Association, the Main Street Retailers, the Board of Governors of Greater Cape City Chamber of Commerce, the Cape City Realtors Association, the Cape City Trades and Labor Assembly, the faculty of Coastal University, the Greater Cape City Ministerial Association, the City Council of Parent-Teacher Associations, the Cape City Human Relations Council, the City Council, and the Cape City Taxpayers' Association.

The endorsement of the Taxpayers' Association was seen as the key success of the endorsement project. In the previous campaign it had opposed the bond issue. When this group submitted its endorsement in late August, the tempo of public support quickened. As B. Carl Haynes noted, "The announced support of the Cape City Taxpayers' Association gave the campaign a great deal of extra news value and prestige."

Person-to-Person Contact

The organized person-to-person contact was handled, for the most part, by the "football teams" and PTA volunteers. In mid-August the football teams began to canvass each household systematically to leave literature, to answer questions, to determine the registration status of each person who was eligible to vote, and to urge registration of those who were not. Once the registration period had passed (in early October), the "football teams" renewed their personal contacts. PTA volunteers, working from the registration lists, manned telephones four nights a week contacting voters. Each person reached by phone was asked if he wanted additional information. In response to such requests, information was mailed. Personal contact was also accomplished in group situations by coffee and coke parties, civic and service club presentations, PTA meetings, and the like.

The Second Poll

During the second week in October a second formal sampling of opinion was made. Again, the personal interview was the method of contact and the sample for the previous poll was used. The major findings of the second poll were:

1. Practically all of the respondents were aware of the impending referendum, knew the date of the election, and knew where they voted.

2. Approximately 60 percent of the respondents indicated they planned to vote.

3. Slightly over 51 percent of those planning to vote indicated they would vote "yes"; 14 percent said they were undecided.

4. The major negative respondents were from certain retired groups, "central city" groups, and labor groups.

5. There was considerable fear concerning the cost of the proposal, and in some sectors the proposal was viewed as a device to promote more racial integration.

6. Over 75 percent of the respondents indicated they had received the school message by means of the direct mailing or through the mass media.

As a result of the poll, the leaders of the campaign decided that in the final two or three weeks of the campaign the communication process should be intensified.

The Final Days

In the final days the following major events occurred:

1. Groups of PTA mothers appear en masse at all political rallies carrying homemade placards urging support of the bond issue.

2. Each school day during the final two weeks, groups of mothers "picketed" at the various schools that were on double sessions, during the change in sessions. The pickets attracted considerable coverage by the local media.

3. During the last weekend in October large signs were placed at each school center that would benefit from the bond issue. Signs were also placed on each site where a new facility would be erected if the bonding authority was granted.

4. Many of the junior and senior high school bands gave the campaign a boost in their half-time performances at football games. The format was simple: As the band formation spelled out "vote" and "bonds," a narrator, using the public address system, urged the people to vote on November 5 and listed the school building needs in the immediate vicinity that would be met if the proposal was approved.

5. During the final week the mothers' telephone campaign was intensified and the "football teams" continued their contacts.

6. On the Wednesday before the Tuesday election, a leaflet stating the tax increase in terms of "pennies per week" was mailed to each registered voter. This coincided with a full page ad on the subject in each of the big dailies.

7. On the Thursday and Friday before election day, a third and final opinion poll was taken. The same sample and contact method was used. The poll results indicated a 52 percent "yes" vote with approximately 35 percent of those polled still not sure about whether they would vote. The pockets of opposition identified in the second poll were still present, and the cost fear still existed.

8. The final weekend was devoted to a push, using the mass media. Full page ads were inserted in each of the local papers. Spot announcements in prime time were arranged with four of the radio stations and each of the three television stations. Each of the television stations also donated time for a half hour program. One program was a documentary on the "hard facts" of the situation (e.g., the half-day sessions, the obsolete buildings, and the cost). The other two were informal panel discussions consisting of three persons each — a public official, a school board member, and a parent.

During the final two weeks of the campaign, leaders in the effort reached a point of indecision concerning election day strategies. They had previously planned to organize a transportation and telephone service to get the "yes" vote out. However, interviewers in the last public opinion poll had voiced the warning that the campaign might be reaching an overkill point with inevitable backlash against the bond election. As one interviewer expressed it, "Several of the voters I talked to seemed somewhat resentful and spoke of being bullied by the board into voting new taxes." Consequently, the strategy group decided not to make public announcements of an extensive transportation service on election day, and some other final week activities that had been planned were curtailed. In the postelection evaluation, many campaign leaders felt that this was a mistake.

The Results

In view of the apparently extensive, well-planned, and well-conducted campaign, the reader might ask: "How could the Cape City bond issue fail to receive the overwhelming endorsement of the electorate?" However, as Superintendent Rickert put it, "In view of our past history, we were naturally gratified by the results. But we did

not regard the outcome as a mandate." He cited the fact that the previous, poorly organized campaign had failed by a 2-to-1 vote. This time, 62 percent of the registered voters of Cape City voted on the bond question, and 54 percent of those going to the polls voted "yes."

The Postmortem

Superintendent Rickert personally insured that appropriate appreciation was expressed (on behalf of Mr. Spears, Mr. Jacobs, and the other key leaders) to the voters, the endorsing groups, the mass media, school district employees, and the lay citizens' campaign leaders and workers. He then focused his attention on evaluating the campaign and outcome. The decision to conduct a careful postmortem study of the bond election was not merely of academic interest. The school leaders had reduced their bond request by $5,000,000 as a result of preliminary conversations with the influentials; therefore, they were aware that within the next three to five years another referendum might be necessary.

Four major approaches were used in reviewing the campaign. First, a precinct by precinct analysis was made of the returns. Second, under the personal direction of Superintendent Rickert, key opinion leaders were contacted and asked informally their perceptions of which techniques had been effective, which had been ineffective, what errors had been made, and why the voters had behaved as they did. Third, a number of active campaign workers were contacted and questioned by the members of the school system staff, primarily about the relative usefulness of the techniques employed. Fourth, a postelection poll was conducted. Since the sample had been personally contacted three times previously, the staff decided to conduct this poll by mail. After two followup appeals, over 92 percent of the sample responded to the two-page questionnaire, which, in effect, was designed to find out if the respondent had voted, how he had voted, and what influenced him to vote and to vote the way he did.

The results of the study produced no great surprises for astute observers who had been "reading the signs." The vote was light and very negative among childless and retired groups. The turnout was rather heavy and generally supportive in precincts heavily populated by middle aged and middle class couples. In affluent areas, the voters turned out well, and the vote was about evenly split for and against

the bonds. In the central city area, the white lower class precincts voted heavily against the issue; this was countered by a fairly strong "yes" vote in the black community. The vote in the Spanish-speaking group was mixed.

The "yes" voters credited the newspaper coverage (including editorials), opinions of friends and coworkers, and public support by the influentials as having the most impact on them. To illustrate the point, one voter wrote on his questionnaire, "Bert Saunders is a smart man who does his own thinking. If he says we had to have the bond money, that was good enough for me." The fear of "too big a tax burden" was a factor in the "no" vote by the aged, childless, and suburban groups. The desegregation issue was still present in the minds of lower class white voters living in the central city area.

The performance of Dr. Moffett's speakers and the telephone campaign were rated quite high. The "football teams" provided a great deal of news value; however, careful study suggested that their effectiveness was hampered by loose organization and lack of orientation. (In several instances "team players" were reported to be poorly informed about the situation.) The television and radio spots were deemed fairly effective. In retrospect, the printed material was evaluated as being too heavy on facts and cost and, with the exception of the foldout, not particularly attractive.

The school officials, following several discussions of the data, reached the general conclusion that a reasonably well-organized campaign using tactics appropriate for the situation had been conducted. However, they clearly recognized that there were several opposition and apathetic groups within Cape City that had not been affected by the campaign strategy.

A Brief Critique

As indicated in the beginning of this chapter, the Cape City case illustrates well how an election campaign should be tailored and conducted to meet the realities of the situation. Previous failures had made it clear to the school leaders of Cape City that a campaign based on an oversimplified grassroots approach would not be successful. Therefore, they planned their proposal carefully, involving both key persons from within the district and outside experts. The opinion leaders were carefully identified, contacted, and informed about the district's needs and problems, and extensively involved in

the planning and carrying out of the campaign. Throughout the dealings with influentials, school officials operated on the basis of principles, conducted themselves with dignity, and did not resort to Machiavellian tactics. There was a broad base of visible citizen involvement in the campaign, and schoolmen worked vigorously behind the scenes. Polls were conducted. A variety of communication techniques were employed. The support of the mass media was sought and quite generally given.

All of these activities contributed to the successful campaign in Cape City. However, in retrospect a few questions on tactics could be raised. For example, was the campaign literature too heavily oriented to details, money, and buildings as opposed to children and their educational opportunities? Should a greater effort have been made to secure more support from certain large groups within the community (e.g., the aged and white lower class)? Was the racial integration issue handled appropriately? Were the data obtained by opinion polls used to the fullest? Were the campaign leaders so infatuated with the "football teams" that they failed to give enough attention to the drudgeries of organizing and orienting team members? What was the reaction of the voting public to having the school bands promote the bond issue and to the mothers' picketing? Did some voters view this as exploitation? (Opinions about these activities were not sought.) Should the final mailed appeal have focused on children rather than the size of the tax increase? Was the most effective use made of television and radio? Did the campaign break down in the final hours when the decision was made to curtail organized efforts to provide voter transportation service and the like? Obviously, answers to such questions are not simple. However, these are matters that the school officials of Cape City would ponder as they prepared for and conducted other election campaigns.

According to Superintendent Rickert, one important generalization was evident, concerning the need for continuous political leadership by school leaders. He voiced the opinion that "we obviously have not effectively conveyed an understanding of our schools to many of our citizens." As a consequence, Superintendent Rickert moved immediately after the election to establish a permanent, operating organization aimed at providing communication with all citizens of the district. "We are no longer following the policy of irrelevancy and isolationism," he said. "Our school leaders will be consistent participants in the destiny of Cape City and of its schools."

8

Review of Key Ideas

This book was written from the point of view that educators must provide active, statesmanlike leadership in the political system. Information and concepts basic to the development of winning election campaign strategies are included in the various chapters. In this final chapter the authors restate briefly the major ideas that dominate their thinking about school election campaigns and that undergird the substance of the preceding chapters.

Political Activity Is Essential

Effective political activity is necessary to influence citizens to make decisions conducive to quality schools. Experienced schoolmen are well aware that desirable change can be opposed more easily than it can be promoted. The social system tends toward equilibrium and does not readily accept change. To say this another way, more power is needed to produce educational change than to resist change. Therefore, political activity is aimed at accumulating and coordinating acceptable uses of as much power as possible in promoting quality school programs.

If educators accept the proposition that well-organized political activity is a necessary ingredient in producing educational change, and the corollary that school leadership has the basic task of making every effort to effect change that improves educational opportunities, the responsibility of school officials in school elections is clear. They must assume a major role in organizing the political forces within the school district for elections. The traditional notion that political activity and school leadership are incompatible must be re-

jected in favor of the proposition that school leadership is enhanced by appropriate and ethical political effort.

The authors find that the concept that school officials must be insulated from political activity is unrealistic. Schoolmen have always had to influence the community in the interest of school improvement. They have often had to provide leadership in school referenda in the interest of better schools. While this book has focused on how to provide leadership in school elections, the significance of continual leadership in all aspects of the school district was also emphasized. Leadership in political activity is a continuous process and should not be restricted to the sporadic efforts associated with intensive election campaigns.

Understand the Political System and Voting Behavior

Local political systems within the United States vary widely. They range from open to closed in quality and from monopolistic to pluralistic. The school official must recognize that the political system within his district is unique, and he must tailor his political strategies to the realities of power within the district. Answers to the following questions must be sought: Who are the influentials within the district? What are their attitudes toward education? What is the relative influence of the several formal and informal groups? What are the behavior norms of the influentials? What means of communication are used among and between influential persons and groups? What latent centers of power might be aroused and organized for school improvement? Is the power structure characterized by openness or closedness? An election campaign that ignores the realities of the existing political system or operates from false assumptions concerning the nature of that system is likely to be unsuccessful.

The voting behavior exhibited is a visible product of the political system of the district and is likewise unique. Therefore, it must be studied and understood. In an effort to provide schoolmen with some clues for understanding voting behavior we have suggested that (1) voting is more likely to be a product of group activity than a highly individual act; (2) many of the subgroups in the power system that mold voter attitudes are likely to be informal; (3) most voters are likely to make up their minds early in a campaign; (4) cross-pressured persons may vacillate, decide late in the campaign how they will vote, or not vote; (5) socioeconomic status may be a factor

in voter preference; (6) personal ties are important determinants of voting behavior; and (7) identification with school leaders, perception of the issues, and attraction to those providing visible leadership in the campaign are some of the psychological variables that cause voters to vote for or against proposals. While these suggestions are not advanced as being universally applicable, they indicate the basic questions school officials must answer about the voters within their school district.

Use a Team Approach in Planning

Modern political activity aimed at winning a school election demands attention to planning and the execution of plans with artful precision. Since political activity is such a complex phenomenon, the planning must involve a team of persons.

The planning team should contain persons who are thoroughly knowledgeable about the local situation and persons with specific expertise. For example, polling is a technical matter. The authors have reviewed the process so that personnel in many school districts can conduct their own polls. However, many school districts may be well advised to seek consultative assistance in polling. A political planning team requires specialists who understand the dynamics of political systems. Someone on the team should have special skill in organizing for political activity. Communication specialists are needed, particularly those who are knowledgeable in "packaging" material for television. Someone on the team should be well versed in the practical art of politics. Various other specialists may be useful. For example, in large school districts where campaigns may be costly, the advice of professional fundraisers may be most beneficial.

The point is that planning an election campaign is complex and requires a team approach. Educators and lay citizens providing different kinds of expert contributions are needed. To aid in the planning, school districts should encourage staff members to develop expertise in various phases of political activity. The thinking of the political planning team can also be improved by using the skills of outside consultants.

Use Outside Assistance

Local school leaders should seek outside expert assistance in organizing election campaigns. Since they are a part of the system that they are seeking to influence, school officials have formed sentiments, attitudes, conceptual norms, and social ties in the system. The practicing schoolmen are more likely to have "tunnel vision" about alternative techniques than outsiders. Persons who become crystallized parts of the system may tend to make emotionalized judgments. This is not undesirable; in fact, it is absolutely essential in building a campaign. But these firsthand, "worm's eye" judgments become even more powerful when balanced with more logically oriented views by persons detached from the system.

It is difficult to advise school leaders on the kinds of persons who can assist in planning, organizing, and conducting a school election campaign. Obviously, they must possess personal characteristics desired of any good consultant. They are not retained to tell the officials of the district what their goals should be. The consultants should not assume that they know all the answers for all school districts. Conceivably, outside consultants could be of assistance in developing the data base and proposal that will be the subject of the school election, making a detached analysis of previous school election results and local voter behavior, objectively identifying formal and informal political power subgroups, assessing voter and leader opinions, organizing the campaign, applying mass media communication techniques, and the like. However, wise school officials will carefully review their own situation and choose consultants consistent with its demands.

Feedback Is Essential

Knowledge of the perceptions and opinions of persons within the school district is an important base upon which campaign strategy can be built. Since public opinion polls are a major device for securing feedback from the voting public, periodic and well-conducted polls are advocated as an important ingredient in election campaigns. Dialogue with influentials, municipal officials, teacher group leaders, mass media personnel, and the like is another means by which school officials can determine what the people think; therefore, time should be devoted to conferring with these persons. Feedback from these sources will supply answers to questions such as: Who are the op-

ponents of the proposal? Which arguments in favor of the proposal are having the most impact? Which of the opponents' arguments are having the most impact? What techniques of communication are most effective? What proportion of the voters favors the proposal? How well does the public know the campaign issues? Obviously, campaign tactics should be adjusted in accord with the data provided by the feedback process.

Have a Broad Base of Citizen Involvement

The team approach advocated for the planning process should continue throughout the campaign. School officials have long verbalized the notions that schools belong to the people and that the public should be actively involved in school affairs. This truism is nowhere more appropriate than in an election campaign. Evidence has been presented that the extent of community involvement is in part a function of the citizens' knowledge of school needs and problems. There is also some evidence that neighbors and friends are a major influence in a voter's decision. Therefore, broad citizen participation in the campaign is urged. This should begin visibly with their contributions in deciding on the proposal to be presented to the voters and should continue through the "get out the vote" effort on election day.

There is one final but crucial point to be made. The ever-recurring nature of school elections in most local districts and the "love them and leave them" tendency of some schoolmen toward the public have been noted. Active, broadly based citizen engagement cannot simply be "turned on" a few months before election day and "turned off" with "thanks" after the votes are counted. It must be continuous. During the campaign, citizen participation is merely more intensified and visible in a given direction.

Learn from Experience

Important concepts from research projects conducted by various groups of scholars have been discussed in several chapters. These concepts are very valuable in planning, organizing, and conducting political campaigns. However, successful political leadership is based on the integration of concepts from research with insights gained from experience in political activity. Consequently, the authors have

emphasized the lessons gained from reported experience as the basic content of Chapter 5.

Educators should record and report their experiences. Reports of significant observations about political behavior in the field of education could build an important body of useful knowledge in the study of educational administration.

There Is No Universal Strategy

There are no universally applicable political strategies for all school districts. The reader must view his own target political system as a unique system. He must exercise selectivity in applying the concepts and techniques presented here because diversity best describes the political systems in which the schools of the nation function. The authors would err seriously if they attempted to project a definitive campaign strategy for any and all school districts of the nation.

School officials should consider acceptable alternative strategies based on a realistic appraisal of the political system of the school district. The strategy selected for a campaign should be the one that meets acceptable ethical considerations and promises the greatest likelihood of success. This selection can be made only by carefully anticipating the consequences of using each alternative strategy proposed for the target district.

Follow Ethical Principles

Exercising selectivity in political strategies does not mean that any political technique should be used as long as it wins the school election. The authors have previously stated their opposition to Machiavellian expediency.

Campaign strategies are like the variety of teaching strategies currently used in the schools of the nation. That students learn and develop differently is a fundamental principle of human development. Experienced teachers have observed great variation in success and failure, using the same teaching strategy with different groups of pupils. No one has accused teachers of being unprofessional for using a variety of strategies for teaching different groups of children. School districts, like persons, differ in the ways they learn and react to stimuli. Thus, there is little logic in pointing an accusing finger at school officials for using morally defensible variations in campaign strategies to influence decisions in the school district.

Politics demands pragmatic thinking. This uniquely American concept of leadership was legitimized and has long been accepted by the followers of such intellectual giants as John Dewey, Boyd Henry Bode, and Charles S. Peirce. Political activity is a deadly serious business. The results of school elections make lasting changes in schools. Since winning school elections is essential to building quality schools, political activity is no place for practicing fuzzy idealism. Pragmatic thinking imposes certain important ethical principles. Not the least of these is projecting the consequences for democratic living of the strategies used in the school district. Does the political activity contemplated contribute to the improvement of democratic governance in the school district? Does it help make voting a viable process for making significant decisions? Does the activity encourage active, effective participation of citizens in education and general government? Does the strategy encourage the emergence of leadership for quality education from all sectors of the population? When specific techniques are being considered, if questions such as these can be answered in the affirmative, the techniques can be ethically defended.

Political activities that are based on deceit, lies, the half-truth, appeals to prejudice, and other undemocratic principles are obviously unsatisfactory. Cheap, gutter political methods (e.g., buying votes, swapping influence, selling out) produce ruinous consequences for the public schools. They sow the seeds of "sick" political systems that in the long run block quality education in a school district. Such tactics are neither advocated nor condoned.

Index

D0559561